EUREKA!

3G

Success in Science

Carol Chapman
Rob Musker
Daniel Nicholson
Moira Sheehan

Heinemann

Introduction

Welcome to Eureka! Success in Science

This is the third of three books designed to help you learn all the science ideas you need during Key Stage 3. We hope you'll enjoy the books as well as learning a lot from them.

These two pages will help you get the most out of the book so it's worth spending a couple of minutes reading them!

This book has six units which each cover a different topic. The units have three types of pages:

Setting the scene

Each unit starts with a double-page spread which reminds you of what you know already about the topic. They tell you other interesting things, such as the place of science in everyday life and the history of some science inventions and ideas.

Learn about

♦ Energy

Most of the double-page spreads in a unit introduce and explain new ideas about the topic. They start with a list of these so that you can see what you are going to learn about.

Think about

♦ Fair tests

Each unit has a double-page spread called Think about. You will work in pairs or small groups and discuss your answers to the questions. These pages will help you understand how scientists work and how ideas about science develop.

On the pages there are these symbols:

Identical twins

These blue boxes in the text revise relevant ideas that you have already met in *Eureka! 1* and *Eureka! 2*.

a Make a list of foods that give you a lot of energy.

Quick questions scattered through the pages help you check your knowledge and understanding of the ideas as you go along.

Questions

The questions at the end of the spread help you check you understand all the important ideas.

When you revise

These blue boxes list the important ideas from the spread to help you learn, write notes and revise.

This shows there is a practical activity which your teacher may give you. These will help you plan and carry out investigations into ideas about science and collect and analyse results and evaluate your work.

 This shows there is an ICT activity which your teacher may give you. You will use computers to collect results from datalogging experiments, or work with spreadsheets and databases, or get useful information from CD-ROMS or the Internet.

 This shows there is a writing activity which your teacher may give you to help you write about the science you learn.

 This shows there is a discussion activity which your teacher may give you. You will share your ideas about science with others in a discussion.

This book also has three revision units: biology, chemistry and physics. They will help you revise what you need to know for the national tests. See pages 86–87.

At the back of the book:

 All the new scientific words in the text in units 1–6 appear in **bold** type. They are listed with their meanings in the Glossary at the back of the book. Look there to remind yourself what they mean.

 There is an index at the very back of the book, where you can find out which pages cover a particular topic.

Activities to check your learning

Your teacher may give you these activities:

Lift-off!
When you start a unit, this short exercise reminds you what you already know about a topic.

Unit map
You can use this to think about what you already know about a topic. You can also use it to revise a topic before a test or exam.

Quiz
You can use the quiz at the end of each unit to see what you are good at and what you might need to revise.

Revision 1
You can use the revision sheets to revise a part of a unit which you aren't so good at.

End of unit test
This helps you and your teacher check what you learned during the unit, and measures your progress and success.

Contents

T indicates Think about spread

How to revise 86

Women in white coats?

Perfumes of Babylon

Many people think of scientists as 'men in white coats'. This is an example of stereotyping, or putting people into broad groups which are not always accurate. In fact there have always been women scientists. As early as 1200 BC, Tapputi Belatekallim and her fellow woman researcher Ninu extracted perfumes from plants. They used the same separation techniques such as dissolving and distillation that we use today.

The fate of Fang

Fang was a Chinese chemist. She lived around the first century BC. She thought that she had discovered a way of changing mercury into silver. In fact she probably used mercury to obtain silver from rocks.

Very few metals are found as the metal element. Most metals are found as rocks called ores. The ore is mined from the ground. The useful parts are separated and changed into the metal by a chemical reaction. This method of extracting silver using mercury was discovered in the western world in the sixteenth century.

Fang's husband tortured her to find out the secret of her discovery. She did not tell him and finally killed herself after going insane. Her insanity was probably caused by mercury poisoning!

A more active role

In the first century AD, Maria Hebraea invented the water bath for heating substances gently in experiments. It still has the French name *bain-marie* named after her.

In western society, it has not always been easy for women to follow their interests in chemistry for cultural or religious reasons. A lot of early scientific research happened in monasteries and the universities were closed to women.

In the eighteenth and nineteenth centuries many women chemists became famous because they helped their husbands. In the eighteenth century, Antoine Lavoisier's wife helped him with his work. By the twentieth century, women could go to the universities and the First World War gave women many opportunities because the men were called to the battle front.

d What problems do you think women scientists faced in the past? Do women scientists face similar problems today?

a Which separation techniques did the Babylonians use to make perfume?

b Explain why modern scientists do not accept Fang's idea about where the silver came from.

c How do you think scientists heated substances before the *bain-marie* was invented?

Maria Hebraea.

2

Marie Curie

The first woman to be awarded a Nobel prize for chemistry was Marie Curie. Marie Sklodowska was born in Poland. In 1891, she travelled from Poland to study at the Sorbonne University in France. Marie gained a good degree in physics and maths and continued with her studies in Paris. It was there that she met Pierre Curie. Pierre was too shy to talk to Marie at first, and he sent her copies of his work on magnetism. Marie continued her scientific work and became a doctor of physics. Eventually Marie and Pierre were married.

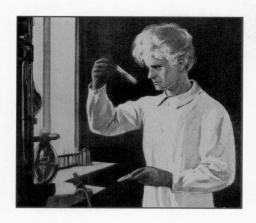

Marie had heard about a chemical element called uranium which is found in an ore called pitchblende. Uranium was unusual because if you put it on a photographic film, it took a photograph of itself. No one understood why. She discovered another element that did this. She called it polonium after her home, Poland.

After four long years, Marie extracted another similar element, which she named radium. She needed a massive amount of rock to extract just a few grains. Marie and Pierre went back to the laboratory at night and found that this new element glowed in the dark!

e Which element is named after Poland?

In 1906, Pierre was killed in a road accident when he was hit by a horse and carriage. Marie carried on with her work in science. She was awarded a Nobel prize for the discovery of the elements polonium and radium in 1911. She died in 1934.

Dorothy Hodgkin

One other woman has received the Nobel prize for chemistry. Her name is Dorothy Hodgkin. At her school, the physics class clashed with cookery, so being female, Dorothy had to do cookery. This was the last time that being a woman got in the way of her career in science. She studied chemistry at Oxford University. She went on to discover the structures of three important molecules including vitamin B12. In 1964, she was awarded the Nobel prize.

Questions

1. Look at the words below. You have met most of them before. Copy and complete the sentences, choosing the best words to fill the gaps.

   element   dissolving   distillation   ore

   a An _____ contains one sort of atom.

   b An _____ is a rock that contains a metal or a metal compound.

   c _____ can be used to separate a pure liquid from a solution.

2. Make a time line to show some of the achievements of women chemists.

3. Imagine you are Marie Curie. Write a letter home to Poland with news of your life in Paris and your work.

1.2 Everyday changes

Chemical reactions

In a chemical reaction, the reactants combine chemically to form new products. There is usually evidence that a chemical change has happened. After a chemical change, you might see:

♦ a colour change, if the reactants are different colours from the products

♦ a **precipitate**, if a solid mass 'falls out' of the solution

♦ a gas given off, such as carbon dioxide or hydrogen

♦ a temperature rise or fall, if thermal energy is released or taken in.

Some chemical reactions are useful, like the ones that happen when substances from oil are made into plastics and even cosmetics. Other reactions such as the corrosion of metals are not useful.

a Look at the photos. They show some everyday situations where chemical changes take place. Spot the chemical changes. For each one, say how you know a chemical change has taken place.

A precipitate appears when sodium iodide reacts with lead nitrate dissolved in water.

Decay.

Cooking.

Combustion.

Glue setting.

Photosynthesis and respiration.

Cars and chemical reactions

A car is made from lots of different materials that have been manufactured using different chemical reactions.

♦ The plastic for the dashboards has been formed from oil.

♦ The glass for the windscreen is made from sand.

♦ The steel for the body contains iron that has been extracted from iron ore.

b Make a list of some of the materials a car is made from, along with the raw materials used to manufacture them.

Rusting

In cars, some of the chemical reactions that take place are useful and some are not useful. Most cars are made of steel. Eventually the steel rusts, because it is a mixture of iron and other elements. Rusting is a chemical reaction. The iron combines with oxygen to form iron oxide, which is rust.

Combustion

When petrol burns in a car engine, the useful chemical reaction is combustion. Petrol is a mixture of hydrocarbons. Hydrocarbons contain only carbon and hydrogen atoms. When petrol burns in a good supply of oxygen, energy is released.

Some of the energy stored in the petrol is transferred to the pistons, which move up and down. The engine transfers this kinetic energy to the wheels of the car.

hydrocarbons + oxygen → carbon dioxide + water

Carbon dioxide in the atmosphere is not toxic, but increased levels add to the greenhouse effect and global warming. Carbon dioxide in the atmosphere is used by growing forests for photosynthesis.

Combustion in car engines is not completely efficient. A lack of oxygen getting to the fuel leads to **incomplete combustion**. This produces poisonous **carbon monoxide**, which comes out of the exhaust.

hydrocarbons + oxygen → carbon monoxide + water

c Which poisonous gas that comes out a car exhaust is produced by incomplete combustion?

Photochemical smog

Carbon monoxide and carbon dioxide are part of the waste gases or **emissions** from a car exhaust. Other emissions from engines, including unburned hydrocarbons, can form a haze in sunshine called a **photochemical smog**. Chemical reactions take place in the smog producing **ozone**, a toxic form of oxygen. Ozone causes breathing problems and harms plants.

New cars have a catalytic converter. This removes some harmful gases from the car emissions. It changes:

♦ unburned hydrocarbons to carbon dioxide and water
♦ carbon monoxide to carbon dioxide
♦ nitrogen oxides to nitrogen.

Photochemical smog in Los Angeles. The smog stings the eyes and makes asthma worse.

Questions

1. Copy and complete the list to show four things you might see when a chemical reaction takes place.

   ♦ _____ – this happens when a solid mass 'falls out' of the solution

   ♦ a _____ change   ♦ _____ given off   ♦ _____ rise or fall

2. Write a word equation for combustion of hydrocarbons:

   a in plenty of oxygen   **b** with insufficient oxygen.

3. Read the text about photochemical smog again.

   a Which compounds does it contain?

   b Which toxic form of an element is present?

When you revise

Virtually all of the materials around us are made by chemical reactions.

Some chemical reactions are useful and some are not. Rusting is not useful, but combustion is often useful to us.

Acids on test

Acids

An acid is a solution of a particular kind of solid or gas in water. Some acids are found in foods and give them a sour taste. Other acids may be corrosive, toxic, harmful or irritant. You can use an indicator to find out whether a solution is acidic. Indicators give different colours with acidic, alkaline and neutral solutions. An acid reacts with a base to form a salt and water.

Useful acids

Extinguishing fires

Fact file

A simple acid and carbonate reaction is used in red fire extinguishers. Inside the fire extinguisher there is a concentrated sodium carbonate solution, a foaming agent and a glass bottle of concentrated sulfuric acid. Squeezing the trigger on the fire extinguisher breaks the glass bottle. The acid reacts with the carbonate to produce carbon dioxide gas, which forces the water out. The foaming solution of carbon dioxide in water puts out the fire.

The word equation for this reaction is:

sulfuric acid + sodium carbonate →
        sodium sulfate + carbon dioxide + water

a Name the gas that puts out the fire.

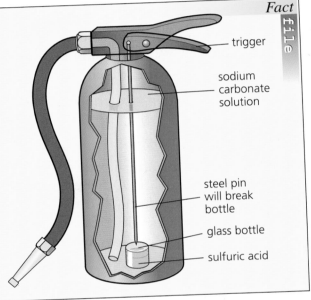

- trigger
- sodium carbonate solution
- steel pin will break bottle
- glass bottle
- sulfuric acid

Manufacturing industry

Fact file

Acids are used to manufacture many different products, including perfumes, glues, plastics, fabrics and fertilisers. Many fertilisers contain nitrogen. They are made by neutralising acids. The word equation for the manufacture of one fertiliser is:

sulfuric acid + ammonium hydroxide → ammonium sulfate + water

b What is the name of the salt formed in this neutralisation?

Stopping rust

Fact file

Phosphoric acid reacts with any rust on the surface of iron or steel objects. This leaves a clean surface that you can protect with zinc, paint or oil.

IRRITATING TO THE EYES AND SKIN

c Name the acid found in rust removers.

Preserving food

Fact file

Bacteria cannot survive in conditions of low pH. Vinegar contains ethanoic acid. It is used to pickle food such as onions and red cabbage.

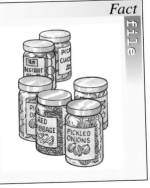

d How do acids help to preserve food?

Acids attack

Corrosion   *Fact file*

Corrosive acids are transported in tankers by road and rail, because they are needed in large amounts for manufacturing industries. If an accident happens and acid is spilled, it will react with metals and other building materials, corroding them. The acid will also corrode any flesh it comes into contact with. Acids should be handled with care. The word equation for the corrosion of zinc is:

sulfuric acid + zinc → zinc sulfate + hydrogen

e Why are large quantities of acids transported by road and rail?

f What does the hazard warning sign on the back of the tanker mean?

Acid rain   *Fact file*

Burning fossil fuels produces sulfur dioxide and creates acid rain. Nitrogen dioxide from car exhausts also dissolves in the rain, forming nitric acid. Acid rain corrodes buildings, kills fish and damages plants.

g Which two acids are present in acid rain?

Acid on the rocks   *Fact file*

Rainwater is naturally acidic because some of the carbon dioxide in the air dissolves in the rain to make a weakly acidic solution called carbonic acid. Over millions of years, naturally acidic rainwater and acid rain have slowly dissolved away limestone rocks. Limestone is mainly made of calcium carbonate, so it reacts with the acid. A general word equation for this reaction is:

acid + carbonate → salt + water + carbon dioxide

h Explain why rainwater is naturally acidic.

Questions

1. Copy the table and complete it to show some examples of reactions that are useful and reactions that are not so useful.

Useful reactions	Not so useful reactions

2. Draw a diagram of a red fire extinguisher to show its internal design and describe how it works.

3. Which acid:
   a dissolves rust?
   b is used to manufacture ammonium sulfate fertiliser?

4. Why have the sculptures and statues on many old buildings been worn away?

When you revise

Reactions of acids are used in fire extinguishers, food preserving and manufacturing industries.

Reactions of acids that are not useful include corrosion and the effects of acid rain.

It's elementary my dear!

Atoms and molecules

Everything around us is made up of particles. An atom is the smallest particle of an element. An element contains only one type of atom.

A molecule is a group of two or more atoms chemically combined together. An oxygen molecule has two oxygen atoms combined together.

Compounds are formed by chemical reactions, when atoms of different elements combine together.

a How many molecules are shown in the diagram?

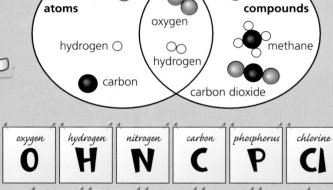

Symbols

We know about 118 elements, and new ones are being discovered all the time! Each element has its own symbol. You can find the symbols on a periodic table. Each symbol is made up of one or two letters. Scientists around the world may speak different languages, but they all use the same symbols.

oxygen	hydrogen	nitrogen	carbon	phosphorus	chlorine
O	**H**	**N**	**C**	**P**	**Cl**

aluminium	magnesium	calcium	sodium	potassium
Al	**Mg**	**Ca**	**Na**	**K**

The first letter of a symbol is always upper case (a capital letter). If there are two letters, the second letter is lower case. Some symbols are easy to remember, as they are the first letter or first two letters of the name of the element. Others are harder to remember because the symbol comes from the Latin name of the element, or its name in another language.

Word game

When different elements combine, they form compounds. It is just like making new words out of letters.

♦ You can make the word 'pea' out of three letters.
♦ Add another letter and you make the word 'pear'.
♦ Use some of the letters more than once and you can make 'appear'!

You can make lots of words out of a few letters.

In a similar way, the atoms of the elements combine in different ways or combinations to make the different compounds around us. Millions of combinations of elements make all of the different substances that exist on Earth, and that humans have made.

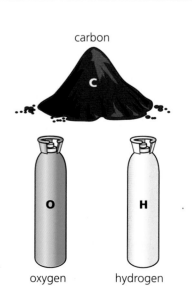

Compounds in short

If you take elements such as hydrogen and oxygen, you can combine them in different ways to make different compounds. All of the atoms in the reactants end up in the products. The symbol for hydrogen is H and the symbol for oxygen is O. The number of each type of atom in a particular compound is always the same.

For example, one atom of oxygen combines with two atoms of hydrogen to make one molecule of water. We can draw circles to represent the atoms in the molecule.

Or we can write the molecule using the formula for water as H_2O. The formula shows the symbols of the atoms in the molecule and how many there are of each kind of atom.

b Look at the drawings of molecules opposite. Write down the formula for each molecule.

c Hydrogen sulfide has the formula H_2S. Draw a diagram of a hydrogen sulfide molecule.

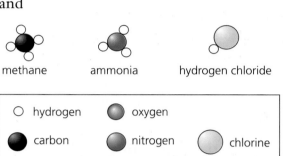

methane   ammonia   hydrogen chloride

○ hydrogen	◉ oxygen
● carbon	● nitrogen	◯ chlorine

Questions

1. Copy and complete the table.

Word	Explanation
Atom	The smallest particle of an element
	A group of two or more atoms chemically combined together
Element	
	This is formed when different types of atom combine together

2. Explain why the chemical symbol for sulfur is its first letter, S, but the symbol for sodium is Na.

3. If you have two black socks and a yellow sock, how many different pairs can you make?

4. Why is the formula for water always written as H_2O?

5. Hydrogen atoms and oxygen atoms do not only combine to make water. They can combine to make a compound called hydrogen peroxide, which has the formula H_2O_2. Draw a diagram showing how you think this molecule might look.

When you revise

Everything is made up of particles. Atoms are the smallest particles of an element.

Elements have only one type of atom. Each element has its own symbol.

Molecules have two or more atoms chemically combined.

Compounds are formed by chemical reactions when different atoms combine together.

The chemical formula of a compound shows the ratio of the different types of atom in the compound.

1.5 Atoms don't change

Mass is conserved

Atoms can combine in different ways, and they are rearranged by chemical reactions. The number of atoms in a reaction stays the same, so the mass stays the same. The photos show neutralising hydrochloric acid with sodium hydroxide solution. The products are sodium chloride and water.

Before and after mixing

a Look at the photos. Explain why both balances are showing the same reading.

Making and breaking up compounds

Mercury oxide …

Antoine Lavoisier discovered that when substances burn they join with oxygen from the air to produce oxides. He did experiments on copper, tin, phosphorus and sulfur, as well as mercury.

He weighed mercury in a sealed flask with a limited amount of air. Then he heated the flask until red mercury oxide formed on its surface. He weighed the sealed flask again. It weighed the same as before. This showed that the reactants at the start of this experiment and the products at the end of the experiment had the same mass.

… is heated …

When mercury is heated in the air mercury atoms combine with oxygen atoms in the air to form a compound called mercury oxide. The atoms are rearranged but the number of atoms and their mass stay the same.

mercury + oxygen → mercury oxide

Lavoisier also heated mercury oxide to a very high temperature. If you heat mercury oxide it breaks down and the products are mercury and oxygen:

mercury oxide → mercury + oxygen

He weighed the mercury oxide at the start. He collected the oxygen given off and the mercury at the end so he could weigh them. He found the mass was the same before and after so mass had been conserved. The photos opposite show this reaction.

b i In Lavoisier's experiments, why does the mass stay the same before and afterwards?

ii What happens to the number of atoms in the experiment?

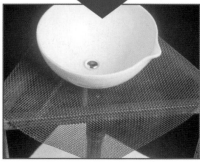

… and produces mercury and oxygen.

Calcium carbonate cycle

The cycle of chemical reactions opposite shows another example of how atoms can be rearranged. Each time the mass of the reactants and products is the same.

c Look at the diagram. Which compound is broken up and then made again?

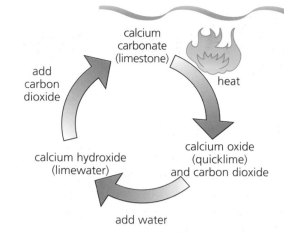

Writing equations

Hydrogen is used as rocket fuel. It burns in air and reacts with oxygen to produce water. The word equation for the reaction is:

hydrogen + oxygen → water

The reactants are on the left of the equation and the products are on the right.

d Which compound is produced when hydrogen burns?

Remember that hydrogen and oxygen atoms both go around in pairs, as molecules. But when they react, one atom of oxygen combines with two atoms of hydrogen.

If you count the numbers of each type of atom on the left of the equation and on the right, you will see that they are not equal. But we know that mass is conserved and so they must be equal on each side. We can make the numbers of atoms the same if we put in two molecules of hydrogen and produce two molecules of water.

Questions

1. Copy and complete the following sentences. Choose the correct word from each pair.

   The atoms are rearranged in chemical reactions, and they **combine/react** in different ways. The number of **compounds/atoms** stays the same in the reaction so the mass is **conserved/transferred**.

2. **a** Which compound did Antoine Lavoisier make and then break?

   b Explain how Lavoisier's experiments show mass is conserved.

3. Look the calcium carbonate cycle. Write a word equation for the reaction that takes place at each stage.

When you revise

In a chemical reaction, mass is conserved because the total number of atoms stays the same.

In a chemical reaction, the atoms are rearranged and combined in different ways to make new compounds.

Chemical reactions can be written as word equations.

A volcano erupts

Mount St Helens

Read the article opposite.

a What was ejected from the volcano?

b Which material oozed out from the volcano?

The inside story

When a volcano erupts, both physical changes and chemical changes take place. Inside the Earth, the rocks are very hot. The deeper you go, the hotter the rocks get. In parts, the temperature is high enough to melt the rocks or to form new compounds.

Molten rock is called **magma**. Magma is a mixture of different elements and compounds. If the magma reaches the surface, it pours out as **lava**. The lava is red-hot but soon cools to form solid rock. A **volcano** is the hole that the magma comes out of.

Sometimes, magma has steam and other gases such as sulfur dioxide and oxides of nitrogen trapped in it under pressure. The pressure builds up gradually. The steam and other gases escape when the magma reaches the surface, causing an explosion. The sulfur dioxide dissolves in water, causing acid rain.

c Think about what all substances are made up of. Use this to explain:

  i where you think the steam comes from

  ii what is happening when rock melts and lava solidifies.

After sleeping for 123 years, Mount St Helens in Washington State, USA, woke up on 20 March 1980. A huge earthquake rumbled beneath it. Seven days later, the first steam explosion blasted a 250-foot wide crater through the volcano's ice-cap. The volcano ejected an enormous column of ash, steam and gas. Lava oozed out, solidifying into a steep-sided dome.

Lava flow

Magma contains a variety of elements, including oxygen, silicon, aluminium, iron, magnesium, calcium, sodium, potassium, titanium and manganese. Some lava contains less gas and is rich in silicon. It is thick and flows slowly. Some lava contains a lot of gas and less silicon. It is thin and flows quickly. In thick lava the gases do not move freely. The pressure can build up, causing an explosion.

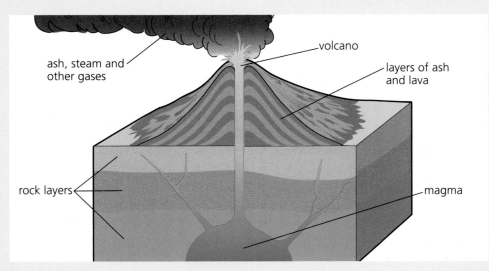

ash, steam and other gases

volcano

layers of ash and lava

rock layers

magma

Sharing ideas

Some students were discussing their ideas about why lava with a lot of silicon it in flows more slowly. Read their ideas opposite

d What do you think? Explain your reasons.

If the lava has more gas particles trapped in it, they will push the other particles apart.

Silicon acts like glue.

It's nothing to do with particles – no one knows if they exist anyway.

Particles are combining and new particles are making the lava thicker.

Time to experiment

Their teacher decided to build on some of their ideas about particles. When we use the idea of particles such as molecules and atoms in science, we call this idea a **formal model**. The model helps us to understand what is happening even though we can't see it.

The teacher showed the sparks, colours and flashes you often see when a volcano erupts.

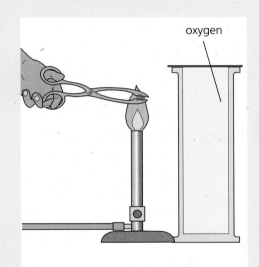

oxygen

♦ She took a piece of iron wool, lit it in a Bunsen burner flame and then plunged it into a jar of oxygen. The iron burned brightly and gave out sparks.

♦ Then she burned a small piece of calcium. This time the flame was red.

♦ Finally, she burned a tiny piece of sulfur. This time the flame was blue.

e What evidence was there that chemical reactions had taken place in the experiment?

Questions

1. Copy and complete these sentences. Choose the correct word from each pair.

   When a volcano erupts, sulfur dioxide is made by a **chemical/physical** change. Gases exist as particles called **molecules/atoms**. The particles in a gas are moving **slower/faster** than the particles in a liquid. The particles in a gas are **more/less** spaced out than the particles in a liquid.

2. The teacher explained how new chemicals are produced when a volcano erupts. She used the idea of particles. Give the explanation you think she would have used.

3. If you shake a can of fizzy drink and then open it, what happens? How do you think this is like a volcano erupting?

4. Can you think of any other situations that remind you of a volcano? Explain your answer.

That's life

Reproduction

There are millions of different species of plants and animals on the Earth. Within each species, some organisms compete more successfully than others for resources such as food, water and space. These organisms are most likely to reproduce and leave more organisms, which become the next generation. The new organisms are called **offspring**.

a Which organisms leave most offspring for the next generation?

Early ideas

In ancient times, people believed that organisms were created out of nothing. The Chinese thought that insects were made out of wet bamboo.

In the fourth century BC, Aristotle thought that men's semen made limbs and organs out of women's menstrual blood. He compared this with how the Earth's rivers and continents have been shaped from matter.

b Which parent did Aristotle think controlled the development of the offspring?

In the seventeenth century, Jan Swammerdam believed that human sperm contained miniature humans. He called this mini-human the 'homunculus' and he thought it took in food from the egg. It gradually unfolded and grew into a fetus. Followers of this theory were called 'spermists'. At this time, Antoni van Leeuwenhoek was the first person to look at sperm under a microscope like the ones we use today. Many biologists were still convinced they could see the homunculus under the microscope!

On the other hand, Regnier de Graaf and his followers were called the 'ovists'. They thought that the egg, also called the **ovum**, contained a miniature human, and that the sperm caused it to grow.

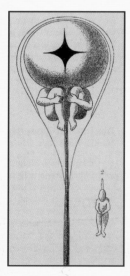

The spermists' model.

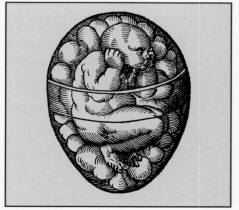

The ovists' model.

Looking for evidence

These beliefs of the spermists and ovists were only ideas. No one could say which idea was the right one, because there was no evidence for either of them.

By the end of the nineteenth century, cells had been discovered and scientists saw fertilisation happening under the microscope. The sperm cell nucleus and the ovum cell nucleus fused together to make the first cell of the new organism. This was evidence that both parents contributed to the offspring.

The sperm cell nucleus fuses with the ovum nucleus to form one cell.

The cell divides into 2, 4, 8 cells, and so on, until there is a ball of cells to form the embryo.

c What was the evidence for the idea that both parents contributed to the offspring?

Mendel's discovery

In the nineteenth century, a monk called Gregor Mendel did many plant-breeding experiments. From these he concluded that features are passed on to the offspring as separate particles from both parents. In 1909, Wilhelm Johannsen called Mendel's particles **genes**.

Cracking the code

In 1953, Francis Crick and James Watson worked out the structure of the substance that makes up genes. This substance is called **DNA**, and it carries instructions that are passed on through the sperm and the ovum. Their evidence came from many experiments and a lot of thinking.

Gregor Mendel.

d What is carried in DNA?

<hr>

Questions

1. Copy the following table. Complete it to show the names of the people and their ideas about reproduction.

Person	Idea
Aristotle	Human semen made limbs and organs out of the menstrual blood of the female.
	Human sperm contained miniature humans.
Regnier de Graaf	
	Features are passed on as separate particles from each parent.
	A substance called DNA carries instructions that are passed on through the sperm and the ovum.

2. Make a time line to show how theories about reproduction have changed.

3. Imagine you are Jan Swammerdam. Write your diary for the day you thought of the idea of the homunculus.

The way we are

Why do we look like our parents?

If you look at the members of a family you will see that although they are all different, they often look similar. This is because some of the same features from their parents and grandparents have been **inherited** or passed on to them.

A baby inherits some features from its mother and some from its father. Genes are the instructions for these features. Genes are inside the nucleus of the sperm and the ovum. So the features of the baby are controlled by genes in the nucleus of both the sperm and the ovum. The sperm and ovum nuclei fuse during fertilisation to form the first cell of the new baby. The baby inherits genes from its father and from its mother.

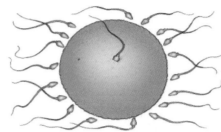

a Explain what genes do.

James thinks that boys inherit their features from their father and girls inherit their features from their mother.

b Explain to James why his idea is wrong.

When a sperm and ovum fuse to form a fetus, there is a completely new combination of genes. That is why children that have the same parents are not the same, except for identical twins, although they may have many similarities. Each baby resembles its parents in some ways, but is not exactly like either of them.

Identical twins

When a sperm fertilises an ovum, the fertilised ovum sometimes splits into two embryos and identical twins are formed. Both twins have come from the same sperm and ovum, so they have the same genes and the same features.

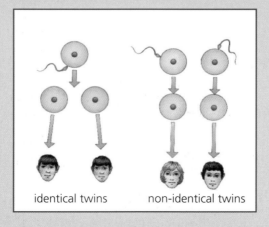

identical twins   non-identical twins

Non-identical twins

If two sperms fertilise two separate ova at the same time, the twins will have different genes and different features. They are non-identical twins. Multiple births of more than two babies happen when more than two ova are produced and fertilised at the same time.

c What is the difference between identical twins and non-identical twins?

Inherited variation

There are genes to control all of your features. Your genes decide, for example, whether you will have:

♦ curly or straight hair

♦ blue or brown eyes.

Some of your features are either one thing or another – there is no 'in between'. For example, you can either roll your tongue or not – try it!

Other features show a range. For example, for height there is a range from very short to very tall with lots of heights in between.

d Think about which visible features of your body you may have inherited. Make a list.

Environmental variation

You might see an example of environmental variation if you spend time working out in the gym. Your muscles may get larger, but you make the variation happen. You don't inherit it. Over the last 50 years, children have been getting taller as food has become more plentiful. Height has been affected by the environment in which children grow up. Birds can learn to imitate sounds they hear. Starlings are well known for imitating telephones. This is a result of the environment they are in, not their genes.

e Think about what features in plants might be affected by the environment. Make a list.

Mixing genes and the environment

Identical twins have exactly the same genes, but they sometimes look different when they grow older. For example, a pair of identical twins may both inherit genes for tallness, but one may have a poorer diet than the other. A feature like height can be inherited but then affected by the environment.

Questions

1. Copy and complete the following sentences.

   We _____ our features from our _____. The information is carried by _____ from one generation to the next. The genes are in the _____ of the _____ and the _____.

2. Draw diagrams and label them to explain how identical and non-identical twins are formed.

3. Two seeds from the same apple were planted in different areas. One tree had large apples, and the other tree had small apples. What do you think caused this variation?

When you revise

A baby **inherits** features from both its parents. These features are controlled by genes.

Identical twins have the same genes because they come from the same sperm and ovum.

Non-identical twins are formed when two sperms fertilise two ova.

Both genes and the environment cause variation between the members of a species.

17

Finding food

Early life

A mammal develops inside its mother's body, and gets all the food it needs from her. Even after it is born, it is fed on milk from her mammary glands. Animals that do not look after their young like this have more offspring at a time. Some of them die, but because there were more of them, some are likely to survive.

Day to day

Some animals adapt their behaviour throughout the day to avoid **competing** with other species for food. Crows and starlings visit dustbins during the daytime, and foxes and cats raid them at night. We call animals that are active at night **nocturnal** animals.

a Which word describes animals that are active at night?

Surviving the winter

A dormouse was one of the guests at the Mad Hatter's tea party in *Alice's Adventures in Wonderland*. You may remember what happened to the dormouse just as Alice was leaving!

b Why was the dormouse so sleepy?

Some animals sleep through the winter when food is scarce to avoid the harsh conditions. This is called **hibernation**.

c Why do some animals hibernate?

Seeds from plants can survive the very cold and dry winter conditions. They are **dormant**, which means 'sleeping'. Seeds will only 'wake up' and start to grow when conditions such as temperature and availability of water are just right. This starting to grow is called **germination**.

d Which word describes a seed that is 'sleeping'?

Migration

Many species of bird spend summer in this country but fly off in the winter to warmer climates where it is easier to find food. This travelling is called **migration**.

Swallows migrate to Africa. The route they take is a straight line which passes through eight countries. They fly in a straight line because this is the shortest route to food, and they need to save energy.

e Name one country that swallows pass through when they migrate.

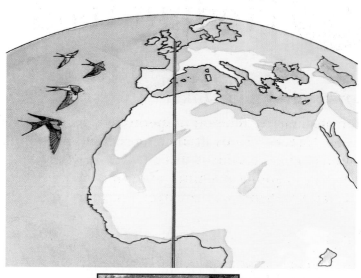

Competing for food

Some animals compete for food with members of the same species, and also with other species. There is more **competition** when conditions are difficult, for example if it doesn't rain for several months and plants cannot grow, or during very cold or very hot spells.

f When is there most competition between animals for food?

Some animal species depend on a different food source from other species, so they don't compete as much. Plants and animals also compete for water, space and light.

Look at the photos. They show greenflies, a woodlouse and a spider. Each has a different food source.

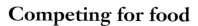

Questions

1. Match each word with the correct meaning to make a sentence. Write down the complete sentence.

Word	Meaning
Competition	means sleeping through winter
Hibernation	means flying to warmer climates
Migration	means starting to grow when conditions are right
Germination	means trying to get the same food source or other resources

2. Find out the names of some animals that hunt their prey at different times of the day. Classify them using these words:

dawn   day   dusk   nocturnal

When you revise

Animals that feed their young have fewer offspring than animals that don't feed them. Being fed by the parents makes the offspring more likely to survive.

There is **competition** between members of the same species and between different species for food, water, space and light.

Organisms adapt their behaviour to reduce competition for food with other species, and to avoid harsh conditions.

Predator eats prey

Competition on Onkar

In any habitat, we find lots of species. The number of organisms of a particular species living in a habitat is called the **population**. Read about a population of gimbuls in *Onkar outback*.

Onkar outback

The moon Onkar orbits the outer planet of a distant galaxy. Conditions on Onkar are very similar to those on Earth. The intelligent life form is the luhans. They resemble humans but their skins are highly sensitive to ultraviolet light. They live in underground cities away from natural light.

On the ground above the cities, the luhans hunt small mammals called gimbuls to eat. The gimbuls feed on grass and the seeds of the red zetta plant in the early hours of the morning before dawn breaks. Most of the ground is covered with thorny hintel bushes. The thorns protect the bushes from being eaten by the gimbuls.

The gimbuls have adaptations that help them to avoid being eaten by their daytime predators, the wooks. They have large yellow eyes at the sides of their heads for good all-round vision. Their fur has green and red patches that camouflage them against the vegetation. They have large, jagged ears. This means they can see and hear the giant wook birds approaching. The gimbuls come out at night and sleep during the day.

The wooks are also adapted for catching their prey. The aggressive wooks have eyes that point forward for targeting their prey as they get ready to pierce them with their pointed beaks and tear them apart with their sharp claws.

A pair of gimbuls nested in a disused overground lift shelter. There was plenty of dry vegetation among the ruins. The gimbuls ate well and reproduced. They were well hidden from the wooks. The number of gimbuls in the shelter grew to a population of 102 after 35 weeks!

Competition

Soon things began to go wrong for the gimbuls in the lift shelter. Death and disease became widespread.

a Why do you think the gimbuls were dying?

There was competition between the gimbuls for the resources they needed, such as food, water and space:

✳ The food was running out.
✳ There wasn't enough clean water.
✳ The shelter was overcrowded and very dirty, so diseases were being passed on.

Even the zetta plants that had not been eaten by the gimbuls were competing for resources, especially for light.

Predation

A wook had started to notice the gimbuls running in and out of the shelter. He was hungry and ready to attack the gimbuls at dusk. Wooks had always eaten a few gimbuls, and the gimbuls now became the main food for the wook. A prey animal that is hunted by another animal for food is the target of **predation**. Only the gimbuls that were the strongest and fastest runners survived predation.

b Which animals were prey?

c Which animals were predators?

A change in population

The table shows how the gimbul population in the shelter changed over 40 weeks.

Time in weeks	0	5	10	15	20	25	30	35	40
Number of gimbuls	2	8	19	34	65	93	99	102	102

Plants compete too

Plants also compete with each other for resources such as space to grow, water, minerals and especially for light. In the Onkar outback, the purple grelip plants flower in the spring. In the summer they die down, when the hintel bushes grow their leaf canopy. This shades the grelip plants and they cannot get enough light to make food by photosynthesis.

Look at the table on the left.

d When did the population growth begin to slow down?

e Which four factors were causing the population growth to slow down?

f Draw a food chain that the gimbuls are part of.

Interdependence

The size of any population depends on competition between the members of that species and also on how many of them are eaten by other species. The different species in a habitat are all **interdependent**. Animals depend on plants for food.

g For what resource do plants compete with each other during the daytime?

When you revise

A **population** is the number of individuals of a species living in a habitat.

An animal that is hunted by another animal as prey is the target of **predation**.

Competition, predation and disease all affect the size of a population.

Prey animals have adaptations such as camouflage, that help them to avoid their predators.

Predators are adapted to hunt by having features such as sharp beaks and claws.

Plants may have adaptations such as thorns to help them avoid being eaten.

Questions

1. Copy and complete the following sentences. Choose from the words below to fill the gaps.

   habitat   competition   compete   resources
   food   space   species   water

   The size of a population is affected by _____. Animals _____ for the _____ they need, such as _____ , _____ and _____ .

2. In the Onkar outback:

   a How do the gimbuls feed?

   b Explain how the gimbul's features help it to avoid being eaten by the wook.

   c Explain how the wook's features help it to hunt the gimbuls.

   d Why are the gimbuls only hunted by the luhans at night?

3. In a field of wheat, the weeds compete with the wheat plants. What resources do you think they compete for?

All down to numbers

Count them!

Look at this simple food chain for a rock pool. The arrows show the flow of energy.

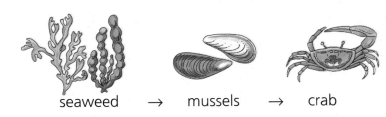

seaweed → mussels → crab

In a day, one crab would eat more than one mussel, and each mussel would eat more than one seaweed plant. If you count the number of crabs, mussels and seaweed plants, you can draw a scale diagram. You can represent the size of the population by a bar, so a bar 1 centimetre long could represent 100 organisms and a bar 2 centimetres long could represent 200 organisms. The diagram would look like a pyramid. It is called a **pyramid of numbers**.

a How long would the bar be to represent 1000 organisms?

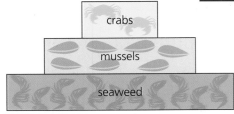

The seaweed plants are the producers, because they produce food by photosynthesis. The herbivores are the first organisms to eat the producers. They are called the primary consumers. The carnivores eat the herbivores. They are the secondary consumers.

b Which organism is the primary consumer in this food chain?

Always that simple?

The diagram for a food chain does not always look pyramid shaped. For example, a single oak tree might have more than 10 000 caterpillars on it. A family of bluetits might prey on these, and one owl might eat all of the bluetits. The diagram for this food chain would not be a pyramid shape, as you can see opposite.

c Why do we get such an odd shape when we try to draw a pyramid of numbers for an oak wood?

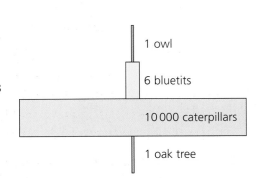

1 owl

6 bluetits

10 000 caterpillars

1 oak tree

Predator and prey numbers

The snowshoe hare is prey for its predator, the Canadian lynx. The numbers of these animals were studied in Canada between 1845 and 1935. The population numbers were estimated from the numbers of furs that the Hudson Bay Company gained from trappers. The graph shows this data.

d Which animal is:

  i the prey?   **ii** the predator?

e Look at the graph. What happens to the number of lynx when the number of hares goes up?

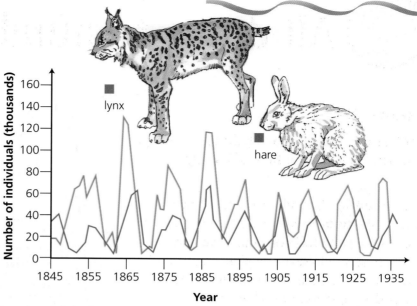

When the number of prey animals goes up, the number of predators also goes up because they have a better supply of food. The pyramid of numbers keeps its shape, it just gets bigger.

Questions

1. Copy the pyramids below. Label them to show which one best represents each of the following food chains.

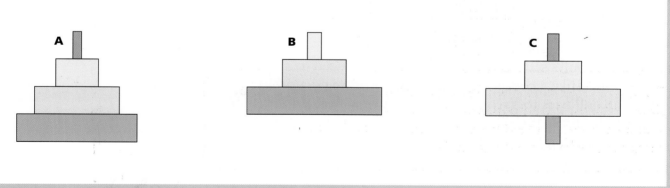

  a grass → rabbits → fox

  b oak tree → caterpillars → robins → owl

  c blackberry bushes → caterpillars → bluetits → owl

2. Use a piece of graph paper to draw a pyramid of numbers for 500 grass plants, 10 field mice and one owl. Use the scale: 1 mm bar width represents 2 organisms. Make all the bars 1 cm deep from top to bottom. Label your pyramid.

3. **a** If the mussels on a beach are poisoned by toxic algae, what will happen to the crab population?

  b What changes might you see on local restaurant menus?

When you revise

If we count the number of organisms at each level of a food chain, we can draw a **pyramid of numbers**.

If the number of prey in a food chain increases, the number of predators also increases.

Another pint of milk

Milk yield in cattle

Like other mammals, the cow produces milk to feed her calves after they are born. The calves do not have to go out and find food. They are protected from predators. The amount of milk a cow produces is called the **milk yield**. Farmers sell milk for a profit, so high milk yield is a **desirable feature** in a cow.

High milk yield is a feature that is inherited from both the bull and the cow. A bull that can pass on high milk yield can be mated with many cows that produce the most milk to make sure that this feature is passed on. New varieties of cattle with higher milk yields are produced. Farmers select the bull and cows that have a feature they want to pass on. This is called **selective breeding**.

a Why is milk yield a desirable feature?

Artificial insemination

Instead of mating a bull and a cow at the farm, scientists at a breeding station may choose a bull that can pass on high milk yield and sell its semen to farmers. The farmer selects a cow with a high milk yield and puts the semen into the cow's vagina through a long tube. We call this **artificial insemination**. The sperm fertilise the cow's eggs.

b What is artificial insemination?

To collect the bull's semen, the bull may be introduced to a frame that is made to look like a cow, with a cow's hide over it and a rubber vagina inside. The bull tries to have sexual intercourse with it, and the semen is collected in the artificial vagina. The semen is frozen in straws until it is needed. The bull never meets a cow!

Collecting semen for artificial insemination.

c How is semen collected at a cattle-breeding station?

Other features

If you select two parents that each have different desirable features, such as resistance to disease or strong legs, you can try and produce new varieties of cattle with all of these features. The wild ancestors of our domestic cattle were the aurochs. They are now extinct, but there are cave paintings of them, like the one shown opposite. When a species becomes **extinct**, it dies out altogether and we lose its useful genes.

d How do we know the aurochs ever existed?

e What do we lose when a species becomes extinct?

A loaf of bread

Wheat is grown to make flour. New varieties of wheat have been produced that give a high yield of grain and are resistant to disease.

f Look at the photos below. How is modern wheat different from wild wheat?

The wheat flower is normally self pollinated. The pollen cell nucleus from the male part of the flower fertilises the ovule cell nucleus of the same flower. A plant with desirable features can be treated with a special chemical. This stops it producing pollen, so the plant will be pollinated by a nearby plant that has also been specially selected.

g How does the farmer make sure that some of the wheat flowers are not self pollinated?

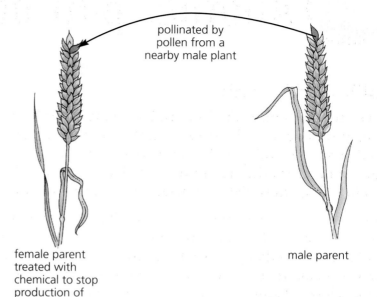

pollinated by pollen from a nearby male plant

female parent treated with chemical to stop production of pollen cells

male parent

Wild wheat.

Modern wheat has been developed from wild wheat by selective breeding.

Questions

1. Match each fact with the best reason. Write down the complete sentence.

Fact	Reason
We can breed cattle with high milk yield	because we can use the best bulls to father calves all over the country
We select the bull and the cow for breeding	because it can be kept until it is needed
We use artificial insemination	because they can both pass on the high milk yield feature
We freeze the semen	because it is a feature cows can inherit

2. Write down the stages of artificial insemination in the correct order.

3. Make a list of features that might be desirable in wheat plants.

When you revise

Desirable features are features you want to pass on.

We can select parents with desirable features to produce new varieties of animals or plants that have these desirable features. This is called **selective breeding**.

Happy families

Boy or girl?

All the information that decides whether a baby is male or female is carried inside the sperm and the ovum. The sperm can have a male Y factor or a female X factor. The ovum can only have an X factor.

If an X factor sperm joins with an X factor ovum to give XX, the baby will be a girl. If a Y factor sperm joins with an X factor ovum to give XY, the baby will be a boy.

a If a couple's first child is a boy, do you think their second child is more likely to be a girl?

Heads or tails?

If you spin a coin, there are two possible outcomes: heads or tails. There is an equal chance of getting heads or tails. If you get two heads in a row, it is called a run of two. Three heads in a row is called a run of three, and so on.

For every baby that is born, there is an equal chance or **probability** of it being a boy or a girl. The possible combinations of X and Y factors are XX and XY. There are two possibilities, just like spinning a coin. If you have four girls in a row, it is like a run of four heads.

b Work with a partner. Put an X sticker on the heads side of a coin and a Y sticker on the tails side. Try spinning the coin 25 times. Write down whether you get an X or a Y each time. Look at your results.

  i What is the chance of getting a Y sperm on the first throw?

  ii If a family has five children, is it likely that they will be the same sex?

Any choice?

The torn and faded pages of a Chinese manuscript tell the story of rich emperor Chan and his wife Jade. Chan desperately wants a son. He is very old fashioned and believes that a son must inherit his wealth. Chan and Jade have five daughters. Chan is hoping for a sixth child – a son. Jade thinks that their family is large enough, and anyway a sixth child might be another girl.

One day, Jade thinks of a plan to change her husband's mind. She makes three types of card.

'My dear husband, only you have the power to decide whether our next child will be a boy. Each of your sperm has either the Y factor for a boy or the X factor for a girl. I can only make the X factor.'

'There are 10 male cards. 5 have the Y factor and 5 have the X factor. There are 10 female cards. They all have the X factor. I will shuffle the cards. You must choose one male card and one female card each time.'

'If you choose:

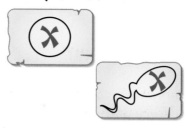

it is the same as having a female child.'

'If you choose:

it is the same as having a male child.'

The emperor makes his first choice:

The emperor puts back the cards. He makes four more choices, and each time the combination is female. 'Fascinating! This is just like our family!' Chan exclaims in surprise.

c What is the sex of this 'child'?

d Do you think this result is surprising? Explain your answer.

The bargain

'Now you must make your sixth choice,' said Jade. 'If your sixth choice is male, I will agree to having another baby, but if your sixth choice is female, our family is complete and all our wealth will be divided between our five daughters.'

e What do you think is the probability of the sixth choice being male?

f Do you think Jade's card game was a good idea? Explain your reasons.

Questions

1. Discuss the sentences below with a partner. Copy and complete them choosing the best words from the list below.

   all   one   half   none   some

   If a man's semen contains 300 million sperm, _____ of them will have the Y factor and _____ will have the X factor. A woman produces _____ ovum each month and _____ of them have the X factor.

2. **a** Estimate the number of ova a woman produces in her lifetime.

   b Why do you think that a man produces so many more sperm than a woman produces ova?

3. The Smith family have three children. The oldest one is a boy and the two younger girls are twins. What do you think is the probability of their fourth child being a boy?

4. If you were to walk into your local hospital and wait for the next 10 children to be born, how many would you expect to be boys and how many girls? Explain your answer to your partner.

3.1 Machines and force

Machines

People use machines to do jobs more easily. Some machines let you lift or move things using less force. The force of the object you are trying to move is called the **load**. If you are trying to lift something, then the load is its weight.

Machines come in many shapes and sizes. Some are very simple. Other machines combine several simple machines in one more complex one.

The development of simple machines

It is difficult to find out exactly when some simple machines were developed. Machines such as inclined planes, wheels and pulleys have been used for thousands of years.

An **inclined plane** lets you lift an object up using less force. People doing removals and deliveries use inclined planes to move heavy items in and out of vans and lorries.

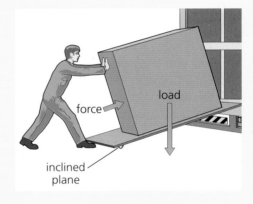

a How would you lift a weight into a van without an inclined plane?

The **wheel and axle** has been used since about 2000 BC. In the grinding machine below, the horse turns the wheel on its axle. The horse moves in a bigger circle than the axle, which makes it easier to turn the wheel.

b Make a list of other machines that use wheels.

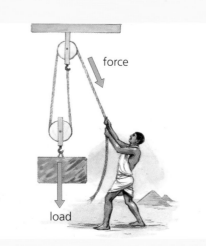

Pulleys were used by the Egyptians around 2700 BC for building the Pyramids. We use pulleys today in machines such as cranes. A pulley uses a rope and wheels to lift heavy objects such as stone blocks. Pulleys are good for lifting things vertically. You need less force to lift the load.

Archimedes invented a screw mechanism in the third century BC to lift water up to water fields. This machine is called the **Archimedes screw**. Turning the screw lifts the water inside the tube higher and higher until the water is at the surface.

force

load

c How do you think people lifted water from the ground before the Archimedes screw was invented?

You have probably seen **gears** on a bicycle. Gears are made up of several cog wheels with teeth which turn each other. Sometimes a chain is used to link two cog wheels. Different arrangements of the cog wheels change the force you need to turn the wheels.

d Explain how the bicycle below would move and how you would feel if you chose:

   i gear **A** on the flat
   ii gear **B** going uphill.

A

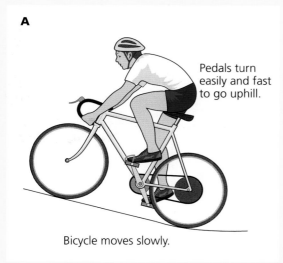

Pedals turn easily and fast to go uphill.

Bicycle moves slowly.

B

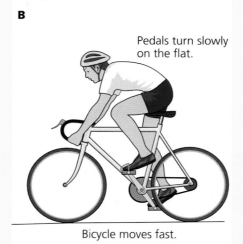

Pedals turn slowly on the flat.

Bicycle moves fast.

Questions

1. Pair up each machine with its description and write down the pairs.

Machines	Descriptions
inclined plane	invented to draw water up from the ground for watering fields
pulleys	used by removals people to get objects onto lorries
Archimedes screw	used to lift objects, such as by the Egyptians to make the Pyramids
gears	made from several cog wheels with teeth that turn each other

2. Explain simply how the following work:
      a an inclined plane   **b** an Archimedes screw.

3. Machines are all around us. Explain:
      a why we use machines   **b** the difference between simple and complex machines.

Where's the pivot?

Pivots are everywhere

Forces can make things move forwards or backwards or stop moving. Forces can also make things turn. Think about a door. It opens around the hinge. A wheel turns around the axle. The **pivot** is the point around which something turns. When you open the door the hinge turns very little but the whole door turns more.

The joints between your bones also act as pivots.

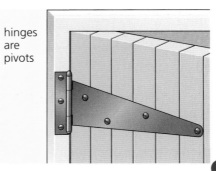

hinges are pivots

a Look at the diagram above. Which joint is working as a pivot?

More distance, less effort

Imagine that you are closing a door. First you try to push it very close to the hinge, as shown in the picture. Now imagine you push the door shut at the handle. This is much easier. The further away from the pivot you are, the less force you need to turn the door around the pivot.

b Why does the woman in the picture find it hard to close the door?

If you have played on a seesaw, you will know that you can lift your friend more easily if you sit far away from the pivot than if you sit close to it.

Holly and Cameron both have the same weight. If they both sit at the ends of the seesaw, it is balanced. But if Holly moves towards the pivot, her end of the seesaw moves upwards. It is unbalanced.

Cameron   Holly   Cameron   Holly

c Why does Holly's end move upwards when she is closer to the pivot?

Levers

Levers are machines that work a bit like a seesaw. You apply a force to one end of the lever. The lever has a pivot and, as it turns, it pushes against the load.

d Look at the pictures of opening a tin and using a crowbar. For each one, say what is the lever and where is the pivot.

For the levers in the photographs, the further you are away from the pivot, or the longer the lever is, the less force you need to move a load. When you close a door by pushing on the handle instead of at the hinges, you are using a longer lever.

e Which tool in each pair opposite would be easier to use? Give a reason for each answer.

Turning effect

Look at the diagram below of a force making a screwdriver turn. The force arrow does not point toward the pivot – the force is to one side. Whenever the force on an object is applied to one side of a pivot, the force tries to make the object turn. This is called the **turning effect** of the force.

The turning effect of a force depends on the size of the force. It also depends on the distance between the pivot and the force arrow. If the force is applied directly towards the pivot then nothing will turn.

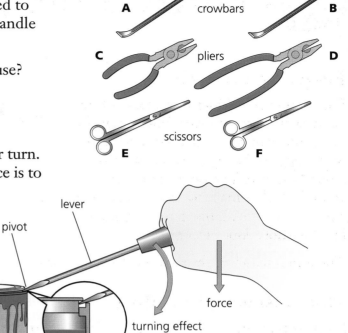

Questions

1. Which of the following statements are true and which are false? Write out the statements that are true.
   a The longer the lever, the bigger the force that is needed to move an object.
   b It is easier to close a door if you push the door close to the hinge.
   c The shorter the lever, the bigger the force that is needed to move an object.
   d The hinge of a door is its pivot.
   e Joints are examples of pivots.
   f Bones are examples of levers.

2. Look at the diagram at the top of the page. Make a labelled sketch to show the pivot, the lever and where you apply the force for:
   a a pair of pliers   b a crowbar   c a pair of tweezers.

3. Use the following words to describe why levers are useful.

   pivot   distance   force   increase   decrease   lever

4. Miranda and Sophie are sitting either end of a seesaw. If Miranda and Sophie weigh the same, what happens when:
   a Miranda sits closer to the pivot than Sophie?
   b Miranda and Sophie both sit the same distance from the pivot?

When you revise

A **pivot** is the point around which an object such as a door or a crowbar turns.

A **lever** turns aound a pivot and pushes against a load.

The **turning effect** of a force depends on the size of the force and the distance from the pivot to the force arrow.

Just a moment

Balanced and unbalanced forces

When the forces on an object are balanced, the object will stay still or it will move at a steady speed.

For something to start moving, or to speed up or slow down, the forces on it must be unbalanced. For example, to start moving forwards or to speed up there must be a greater forwards force than the backwards force.

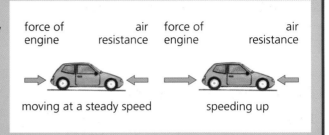

force of engine — air resistance — force of engine — air resistance

moving at a steady speed — speeding up

A balancing act

To turn something around a pivot, the turning effects of the forces on it must be unbalanced. Cameron is leaning on the rotating door. Mahir is leaning on it with a larger forcer in the opposite direction, so the door is turning. There is an **unbalanced turning effect**.

a Which way will the door turn, away from Cameron or away from Mahir?

Sometimes the turning effects may be balanced. Now Cameron is pushing on the rotating door in one direction and Holly is pushing against him in the opposite direction with the same force. The forces are balanced. Their two forces have a **balanced turning effect** on the door. The door does not turn!

b Look at the two diagrams of people pushing on the rotating doors. What can you say about the distance from the pivot that they are pushing?

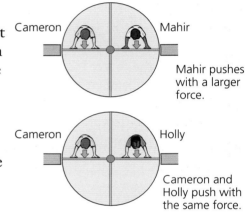

Cameron — Mahir

Mahir pushes with a larger force.

Cameron — Holly

Cameron and Holly push with the same force.

Watch the clock

Look at these two clocks. On clock **A**, the hands are going round the way we usually see. We say they are turning **clockwise**. On clock **B**, the hands are going the opposite way from normal. They are turning **anticlockwise**.

Moments

The turning effect of a force is also called the **moment** of the force. The size of the moment depends on both the size of the force and the distance from the pivot to the force arrow.

Cameron is pushing anticlockwise on the door.
Holly is pushing clockwise on the door.

When Cameron and Holly push the door, their pushes are balanced and the door does not move. Cameron's anticlockwise moment is equal to Holly's clockwise moment. When the door is not turning:

the anticlockwise moments = the clockwise moments

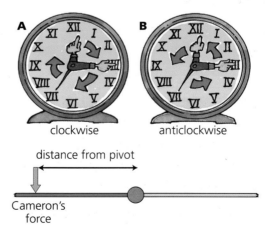

A — **B**

clockwise — anticlockwise

distance from pivot

Cameron's force

c Holly pushes with the same force as Cameron and the same distance from the pivot. Is the moment of her force the same size as Cameron's, or bigger, or smaller?

d i In which direction is the moment of Cameron's force acting?

ii In which direction is the moment of Holly's force acting?

Balanced moments

Cameron and Holly are sitting on a seesaw. They are the same weight and sit the same distance from the pivot. This means the moments on either side of the pivot are the same, so Cameron and Holly balance and the seesaw doesn't move.

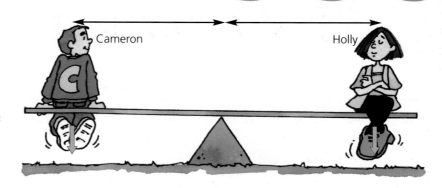

Unbalanced moments

Mahir is heavier than Cameron. They are sitting the same distance from the pivot. Remember that the size of each moment depends on the force applied and the distance from the pivot to the force. Look at the diagram opposite.

e Which moment is bigger, Cameron's or Mahir's?

f Are the anticlockwise and clockwise moments the same?

g How could Cameron move to balance the seesaw?

Questions

1. Write out each term along with its correct description.

   Terms
   moment   balanced system   unbalanced system

   Descriptions
   anticlockwise moments = clockwise moments

   two boys of different weights sit opposite each other on a seesaw, both the same distance from the pivot

   the turning effect of a force

2. **a** What is the moment of a force?

   b What happens when the anticlockwise moment is the same as the clockwise moment?

3. Mike sits at one end of a seesaw and balances Ken at the other end. Both of them weigh the same. What can you say about:

   a the distance the two boys are from the pivot?

   b the size of the anticlockwise and clockwise moments?

When you revise

The turning effect of a force is called the **moment** of the force.

The size of the moment depends on both the size of the force and the distance from the pivot to the force arrow.

When two moments are balanced, an object will not move because:

the anticlockwise moments
=
the clockwise moments

Using moments

Moments in life

As we have seen, a lever turning round a pivot is a simple machine that can be very useful to us in everyday life. We can look at the size of the moments and which way they are turning to understand how and why everyday machines work.

A lever is like a seesaw: there are clockwise and anticlockwise moments. You can see these in the diagram above. A small force on a long lever can balance a large force on a short lever. The result is that the moments on both sides balance.

A beam balance is like a seesaw. We can check it will balance by doing a simple calculation. The calculation uses the equation:

$$\text{size of a moment} = \text{force} \times \frac{\text{distance}}{\text{from pivot}}$$

On the anticlockwise side there is a force of 2 and the distance from the pivot is 3. The anticlockwise moment is 6.

On the clockwise side there is a force of 3 and the distance from the pivot is 2. The clockwise moment is 6.

The anticlockwise moment and the clockwise moment are both the same, so the beam will balance.

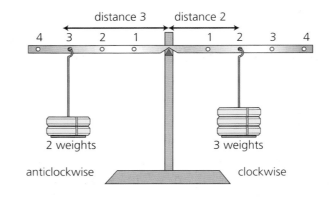

Anticlockwise moment of person's push	Clockwise moment of rock's weight
Small force	Large force
Long distance	Short distance

Counterbalance

We have seen how moments working in opposite directions can be either balanced or unbalanced. The idea of moments is important to people who use cranes in building sites or when loading ships. The photo shows a crane picking up a heavy weight from the ground. The crane has a large weight called a **counterbalance** at the other end of the arm. This helps to balance the load the crane is going to pick up and stops the crane falling over. We can check the counterbalance will balance the load the crane picks up by doing a calculation.

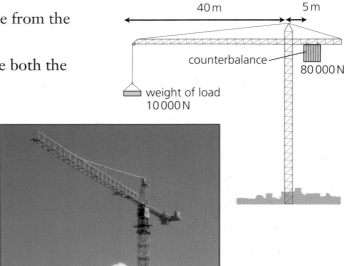

We measure force in newtons and distance in metres, so the units for a moment are **newton metres** ($N\,m$).

For the anticlockwise side of the crane the force is $10\,000\,N$ and the distance is $40\,m$.

For the clockwise side the force is $80\,000\,N$ and the distance is $5\,m$.

The calculation opposite shows the crane will balance.

anticlockwise $=$ clockwise
$10\,000\,N \times 40\,m = 80\,000\,N \times 5\,m$
$40\,0000\,N\,m$ $= 40\,0000\,N\,m$

Gymnasts need to balance their weight when they are doing beam or ring exercises. They use different parts of their body to balance them for different moves. Look at photos **A** to **C** opposite.

a Which parts of each gymnast's body are balancing each other?

Human pivots

In your body, the points where the bones meet are called joints. The joints are the pivots for the bones to turn around. The levers are the bones. Long bones make good levers.

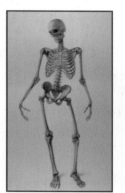

b Look at the skeleton and list as many places as you can where there are pivots.

Lifting safely

It is very important to lift and move objects safely. To reach down to the object you want to lift, you must bend your knees. Then use your knees and hips as pivots to help you straighten up, as shown in the photos. Don't just bend your back down to pick up the object. Bending the back puts a big force directly on the back and can damage it.

Questions

1. Write a paragraph about how to lift objects safely using the following words:

   bend   pivots   knees   back   damage

2. Explain the following statements.

   a Gymnasts balance themselves during beam and ring exercises.

   b Cranes are balanced when they pick up heavy objects.

3. If a crane has an anticlockwise moment of $120\,000\,N\,m$:

   a What is the size of the clockwise moment if the crane is balanced?

   b What is the minimum weight of the counterbalance to stop the crane toppling over if it is $10\,m$ from the pivot?

When you revise

Moments can be used to explain many everyday situations.

A **counterbalance** is a weight which stops something falling over.

Forces and pressure

Sinking feeling

Karl and Jackie are both the same weight. They are pushing onto the snow with the same force. Karl's boots sink into the snow while Jackie's feet stay on the surface and do not sink.

Jackie is wearing snowshoes so her weight has been spread out over a larger area. We say that the **pressure** under Jackie's feet is lower than the pressure under Karl's feet.

large area   small area

same weight   same weight

Pressure at the sharp end

When you push a drawing pin into a board, the pressure from your thumb on the drawing pin is higher at its sharp end.

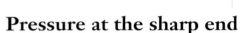

a Why does the pin go into the board?

The pressure at the sharp end is very high because the area is so small. The pin is able to move into the board.

b Why do the camels in the second photo find it easy to walk on sand?

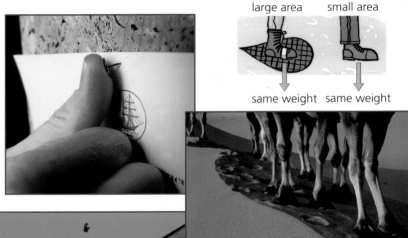

The area of contact between a sharp knife and a piece of cheese is very small. This means that the pressure is very high. The knife is able to cut into the cheese quite easily.

c Explain why a knife does not cut very well when it is blunt.

What is pressure?

You can see from the examples above that pressure depends on the force applied and the area that it is applied to. For the same force:

♦ if the area gets bigger, the pressure gets smaller
♦ if the area gets smaller, the pressure gets bigger.

The block in the diagram is lying on its side with its largest face on the floor. The area of this face is 10 m² $(2 \, \text{m} \times 5 \, \text{m})$.

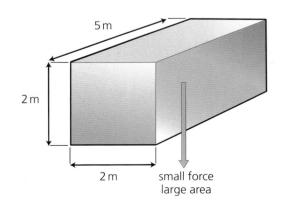

5 m

2 m

2 m

small force
large area

Now the block is placed on its end. The area of this face is $4\,m^2$.
The force is the same because the block's weight has not changed.

d What do you think has happened to the pressure under the block?

e Think about an elephant and a woman wearing a pair of stiletto heels. Which do you think exerts the greater pressure? Explain your answer.

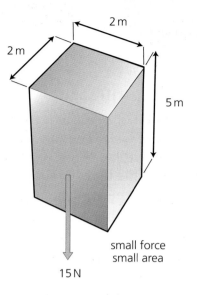

small force
small area

15 N

You probably found it hard to decide for sure which exerts the greater pressure, because the elephant and the woman have different weights and also have different areas in contact with the floor.

We can calculate the pressures for the elephant and the woman if we know their weights and the area of their feet.

- The elephant weighs $60\,000\,N$. The area of its feet is $0.8\,m^2$.
- The woman weighs $600\,N$. The area of her shoes is $0.005\,m^2$.

Pressure depends on force and area, so we can use this equation:

$$\text{pressure} = \frac{\text{force in N}}{\text{area in m}^2}$$

Pressure is measured in units called **newtons per square metre** (N/m^2).

$$\text{pressure under the elephant} = \frac{60\,000\,N}{0.8\,m^2} = 75\,000\,N/m^2$$

$$\text{pressure under the woman} = \frac{600\,N}{0.005\,m^2} = 120\,000\,N/m^2$$

f Which exerts the greater pressure, the elephant or the woman? Are you surprised?

Questions

1. Copy and complete the sentences below.
   If the area stays the same but:
   a the force gets bigger, then the pressure gets _____
   b the force gets smaller, then the pressure gets _____.

2. Explain why wading birds that live on sand and mudflats have large feet.

3. Explain why the wheels of a tractor need to be large and wide but the blades on the plough it is pulling are very thin. Use the word 'pressure' in your answer.

4. Explain why people can lie down on a bed of nails without getting hurt.

When you revise

The **pressure** depends on the force exerted by an object and the area over which the force is spread.

For a given force, if the area gets bigger the pressure gets smaller, and if the area gets smaller the pressure gets bigger.

Pressure in liquids

The big squeeze

Look at the diagram showing two syringes filled with water. They are joined together by a plastic tube. When plunger **A** is pushed in, the liquid is put under pressure. Plunger **B** is pushed out. The pressure is the same throughout the liquid. The pressure on plunger **B** is the same as the pressure on plunger **A**. The two syringes are the same size, so the force on plunger **B** is the same as the force on plunger **A**.

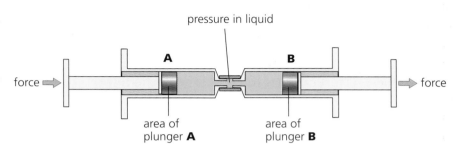

pressure in liquid

force

A B

force

area of plunger **A**

area of plunger **B**

In a liquid the particles are touching each other. You cannot squash a liquid. When you put a liquid under pressure by squeezing it, the particles cannot move together so the pressure is the same throughout the liquid.

a Draw two particle diagrams showing the particles in a liquid before and after you squash it.

Different sizes

Think what would happen if the two plungers were different sizes. The pressure is still the same throughout the liquid, but the force on each plunger is different. Look at this example.

Plunger **A** is pushed in with a small force which is spread over a small area. The pressure is the same throughout the liquid. Plunger **B** has a larger area, but it has the same pressure as plunger **A**.

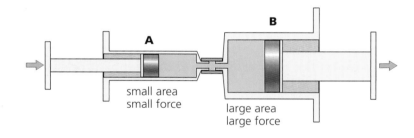

B

A

small area
small force

large area
large force

Because the pressure stays the same, a small force on a small area causes a large force on a large area.

b Is the force on plunger **B** bigger or smaller than the force on plunger **A**?

Hydraulics

The two syringes make up a type of machine called a **hydraulic machine**. The liquid-filled syringes are called **cylinders** and the moving plungers are **pistons**. If a small force is applied to a small piston in an input cylinder, a much larger force can be produced on a larger piston in a cylinder connected to the input cylinder by a tube. If the area of the output piston is twice the area of the input piston, then the output force will be twice as big as the input force.

Many machines use hydraulics to move and lift heavy things. You can see some of the cylinders on this photo of a digger.

c What can a hydraulic machine do to an input force?

Water pressure

In these hydraulic machines we thought about squeezing a liquid, which applies a pressure on it from outside. But a liquid also has its own pressure inside it because of its weight. If you swim deep down in a swimming pool, sometimes this pressure makes your ears hurt. The deeper you go, the heavier the weight of water there is over you, pushing on you in all directions. This pressure is called **water pressure**.

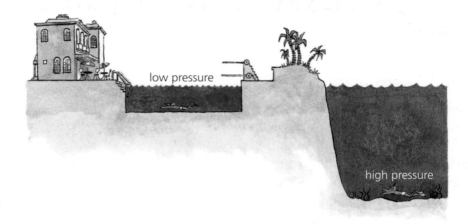

You can see the effect of water pressure in the photo. The pressure at the top is lowest so the water is forced out gently. The pressure at the bottom is higher so the water is forced out more strongly.

Submarines have very thick strong walls so they can stand the water pressure when they dive down deep. When you get to 10 000 m under the ocean, the pressure is equivalent to about eight elephants standing on one plate!

Questions

1. Write out each term along with its correct description.

   Terms

   hydraulic system   water pressure   liquid   piston

   Descriptions

   cannot be squashed because the particles are already touching

   the force on it depends on its area and the pressure

   the pressure water has because of its own weight

   uses pressure in liquids, which is the same in all directions

2. Write a paragraph about water pressure using the following words:

   weight   top   bottom   swimming pool   submarine

3. An engineering company is trying to find new customers for its cylinders. Make an advertisement explaining the uses of hydraulic systems and how they work.

When you revise

Liquids cannot be squashed. The pressure in a liquid is equal in all directions. A **hydraulic machine** uses this property of liquids.

If a small force is applied to a small input **piston**, a much larger force can be produced on a larger piston connected to it.

Pressure in gases

Squashing gases

If you have ever played with a bicycle pump, you know what happens if you put your finger over the hole and then push the plunger in. You can push the plunger in a little even though the air can't escape. You squash the air inside. You can do this because there are big spaces between the particles in a gas, and the particles move closer together when you squash a gas.

When you squash a gas its volume decreases. But the number of gas particles doesn't change. When the volume goes down, the pressure goes up. When the volume goes up, the pressure goes down.

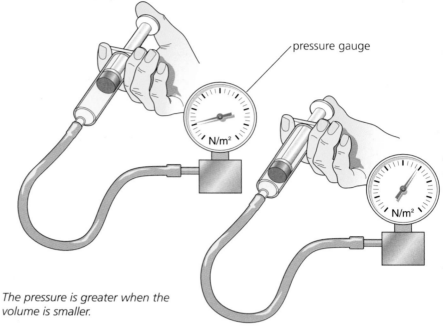

The pressure is greater when the volume is smaller.

When the gas particles are squashed into a smaller space, more of them hit the sides of the container more often. This means they exert more pressure on the container.

The pressure also goes up if you pump more air into a fixed volume, because there are more gas particles squeezed together.

Releasing pressure

If you squash a gas into a small volume and then release it, it expands quickly to a larger volume again. Imagine letting the air out of a bicycle tyre. The air gushes out until the pressure inside the tyre is the same as the air pressure outside the tyre. The same happens when a tyre or a balloon is punctured. The air gushes out to fill a larger volume and the pressure decreases until it is the same as the air pressure outside.

This expansion of gases is used in aerosols of whipped cream. Inside the can is a mixture of cream and carbon dioxide under pressure. When you push down on the nozzle, the volume gets bigger because the carbon dioxide is able to move into all the space outside the can, so the carbon dioxide expands very quickly. A little of the gas rushes out very quickly, carrying the cream with it.

a Draw two particle diagrams showing the particles in a gas before and after the gas is squashed.

b When you pump up a bicycle tyre, does the pressure in the tyre go up or down?

Pneumatics

The sudden expansion of a squashed gas is also used in machines that use cylinders and pistons, similar to hydraulic machines. Machines that use compressed (squashed) gas in cylinders and pistons are called **pneumatic machines**. 'Pneumatic' comes from the Greek word for air or breath.

A pneumatic drill has a very fast-moving piston that can move many times a second. It is used for breaking up pavements and drilling holes. Air is forced at high pressure into a cylinder. The air expands and pushes the piston down. The piston hits the drill bit and forces it down into the pavement.

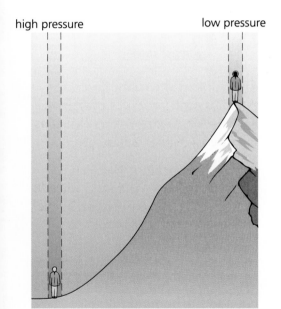

high pressure   low pressure

Air pressure

Like water, air has its own pressure which is called air pressure. The air pressure changes with depth like water pressure does. On the ground at sea level, the air pressure is greatest because there is a large weight of air above you, pushing down. The higher up in the air you go, the lower the pressure becomes, because the weight of air gets less.

On high mountains the air pressure is half as much as at sea level.

c Explain why mountaineers take oxygen cylinders with them up into high mountains.

When you revise

Gases can be squashed because there is space between the particles. When squashed, the volume goes down and the pressure goes up. When a squashed gas is released, the volume goes up and the pressure goes down.

The fast expansion of released gases is used in aerosols and **pneumatic machines**.

Questions

1. What do the following words mean?
   a air pressure   **b** pneumatics

2. Explain how:
   a a bicycle pump works   **b** a pneumatic drill works.

3. The local university wants more students to take its pneumatics course. Produce a leaflet for them explaining the importance of air pressure in our everyday lives. You could include these examples: pneumatic drills, bicycle pumps, tyres and space suits.

3.8 Getting balanced

Number balances

Mustapha was using a beam balance. He wondered why it balanced sometimes but not at other times. He experimented with 1 N weights. When the beam is balanced, it is in **equilibrium**.

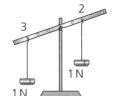
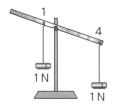

a Look at the diagrams above. What four variables affect whether the beam is in equilibrium?

More than one weight

Next Mustapha decided to use more than one 1 N weight on each side and see what happened. He made a table to show what combinations of weights he used to balance the beam.

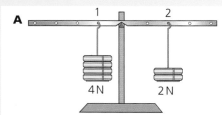
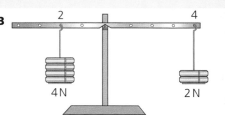

	Left-hand side		Right-hand side	
	Distance	**Weight in N**	**Distance**	**Weight in N**
A	1	4	2	2
B	2	4	4	2

Mustapha then decided to use 4 N and 8 N weights. He made another table to show the ways he found of balancing the weights.

	Left-hand side		Right-hand side	
	Distance	**Weight in N**	**Distance**	**Weight in N**
A	1	8	2	4
B	2	8	4	4
C	2	4	1	8
D	4	4	2	8

Mustapha took a 2 N weight for the left-hand side and a 3 N weight for the right-hand side. He tried out some different combinations to see if they balanced. He made this table.

	Left-hand side		Right-hand side	
	Distance	**Weight in N**	**Distance**	**Weight in N**
A	1	2	1	3
B	2	2	1	3
C	3	2	2	3
D	4	2	3	3

b Look at the input and outcome variables in balance **A**. What happens to make the two sides balance?

c Look at balance **B**. Does the relationship you found work for this one too?

d Do the combinations Mustapha found follow the relationship you described in question **b**?

e Which row do you think will give a combination that will balance? Give a reason for your choice.

f Mustapha started row **E** with a 2 N weight at a distance of 5. Write row **E** of his table following the relationship.

g Look at these two balances. To make them balance, what weight would you hang:
i at 4?   **ii** at 2?

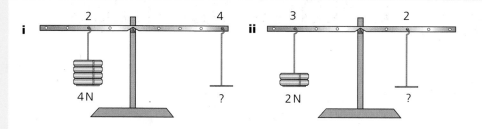

Variables

As you have discovered, the combination of distance and weight on the left-hand side of the beam has to equal the combination of distance and weight on the right-hand side of the beam. This means a moment has two input variables which you can change, distance and weight, for each side of the balance.

There are many situations in life where you can change a combination of two variables.

Soft sand

Ginny and Jenny are identical twins. They both weigh the same. Ginny found it easy to walk along the soft sandy beach in her flip-flops, while Jenny sank into the sand in her high-heeled shoes.

h What two variables affect whether Ginny and Jenny may sink into the sand?

Equilibrium

For Ginny and Jenny, the pressure under their feet depends on both the area and the force they exert. If they change either the area or the force, then they change the pressure too. To work out whether the pressure under their feet stays the same, like keeping the balance in equilibrium, you have to think about both the area and the force.

i Ginny wants to keep the pressure the same while she carries her little brother across the sand. What would she need to change, and how?

j Jenny's brother is lighter than Jenny and exerts less force, but he wants to exert the same pressure as Jenny. What would he need to change in relation to Jenny, and how?

Questions

1. A balance has five holes on either side. Think of all the combinations on the right-hand side that might balance a 4N weight on hole 5 on the left-hand side.

2. What two variables affect:
   a speed?   **b** moments?
   c pressure?   **d** density?

3. Explain what is meant by 'equilibrium'.

Finding the pattern

A multitude of elements

Before 1860, discovering an element made you famous. At this time, 61 different elements were known, each with its own type of atom. Some elements were solids, some liquids and some gases. Some elements were metals and others were non-metals. Scientists struggled to find any order or patterns in the elements.

In 1860, there was the first international meeting for scientists studying chemistry. During the meeting, one scientist reminded the others that different atoms had different masses. Some of the scientists started putting the elements in order using the mass of their atoms. Hydrogen, with the lightest atoms, was first. Lithium, with the next lightest atoms, was second. These scientists rushed home after the meeting, each keen to find the pattern that explained the elements. The race had started!

Finding a pattern

One of these scientists was Dmitri Ivanovich Mendeleev. He made a card for each element. On each card he wrote the element's name, its symbol and the mass of its atoms. He then arranged the cards by the mass of the atoms, with hydrogen first and lithium second. Mendeleev then looked for patterns using the cards.

His first problem was hydrogen, the first card. Hydrogen was strange and very different from other elements. Mendeleev decided to leave out hydrogen. The pack of cards now started with lithium (Li).

He dealt the cards out until he reached sodium (Na). Sodium is like lithium. Mendeleev started a new row with sodium, placing it below lithium. He then dealt the rest of the row.

Then he came to potassium (K), which is like lithium and sodium. He put potassium under sodium. Mendeleev had found a pattern, with similar elements in columns. He called each column a group.

a Which card did Mendeleev put to one side because the element was so unusual?

b Why did Mendeleev start the second row with sodium?

Inspiration

The pattern was less clear after calcium, but Mendeleev did not give up. He had his next big idea. He thought there might be gaps, because not all the elements had been discovered. He put elements under similar elements, even if it meant leaving a gap. Mendeleev's table is shown opposite. He first showed it to scientists in 1869. The red parts of the table are very like part of the periodic table we use today.

I	II	III	IV	V	VI	VI	VIII
H							
Li	Be	B	C	N	O	F	
Na	Mg	Al	Si	P	S	Cl	
K Cu	Ca Zn	gap gap	gap Ti	As V	Se Cr	Br Mn	Fe Co Ni
Rb Ag	Sr Cd	In Y	Sn Zr	Sb Nb	Te Mo	I gap	Ru Rh Pd

c   Why did Mendeleev leave gaps in his table?

Making predictions

Mendeleev used his periodic table to make predictions. His most famous prediction was about the element missing from the yellow gap in the table. In 1871, Mendeleev predicted the mass of the missing element's atoms, and the compounds the element would make. In 1885, a new element was discovered. This new element was exactly as Mendeleev had predicted.

d   How long was it before Mendeleev's prediction was shown to be true?

Questions

1. Look through the list of events, and write them in the correct order. The first and last events are in the correct places. **A–H** need rearranging.

   He made over 60 cards, each with the name and the atomic mass of one element.

   A He dealt the first row of cards.

   B He set the card for hydrogen aside.

   C He fitted in the rest of the elements and published his table.

   D He made predictions about missing elements in his table.

   E He realised that he could have gaps, because not all the elements were known.

   F He realised that sodium was like lithium, so he put the card for sodium under the card for lithium.

   G He arranged the cards in increasing atomic mass.

   H He realised that potassium was like lithium and sodium, so he started the third row with potassium.

   The missing elements were discovered and were just as Mendeleev predicted.

2. Imagine you are Mendeleev. You are going to a conference to give a talk to other scientists. The title of the talk is 'My periodic table: an important new way of looking at elements'. Make a list of bullet points that would prompt you to say the most important things you need to tell them, in the correct order.

4.2 The modern periodic table

The present situation

← groups →

0

		I	II												III	IV	V	VI	VII	He
1								H												He
2		Li	Be												B	C	N	O	F	Ne
3		Na	Mg												Al	Si	P	S	Cl	Ar
4		K	Ca		Ti	V	Cr	Mn	Fe	Co	Ni	Cu	Zn		Ge	As	Se	Br	
5		Rb	Sr	Y	Zr	Nb	Mo		Ru	Rh	Pd	Ag	Cd	In	Sn	Sb	Te	I	
6		Cs							Pt	Au	Hg			Pb				

periods

☐ group I and group II metals   ☐ other metals   ☐ non-metals

☐ transition metals   ☐ elements that sometimes behave like a metal and sometimes behave like a non-metal

We now know of 118 elements. The periodic table we use today has a place for each of these 118 elements. The horizontal rows are called periods. A vertical column is called a group. The diagram above shows the top part of the table. The **red** and **black** symbols show the elements in Mendeleev's table. The **blue** symbols are other elements mentioned in this book.

a Is fluorine (F) a metal or a non-metal? Which group is it in?

b Is aluminium (Al) a metal or a non-metal? Which period is it in?

c Suggest which elements have these symbols:

i O   **ii** C   **iii** H   **iv** Cl.

Metallic or non-metallic?

Most elements are either metals or non-metals. The metals are to the left of the periodic table, and the non-metals are to the right. The properties of metallic and non-metallic elements, and how you can tell them apart, are revised in the table.

Property	Metallic element	Non-metallic element
Conducts electricity?	Conducts well	Conducts poorly (except graphite)
Conducts thermal energy?	Conducts well	Conducts poorly (except graphite)
Appearance	Shiny	Not shiny
State at room temperature	Solid (except mercury)	Some solids (e.g. sulfur), some liquids (e.g. bromine), some gases (e.g. oxygen)
Behaviour when pulled or bent	Pull into wire (**ductile**), push into sheets (**malleable**)	Solids break when hit or pulled

Groups

Elements in a group are similar to each other. On the far left of the table is **group I**, which includes lithium (Li), sodium (Na) and potassium (K). The group I elements are similar in many ways.

- They are all metals.
- They are soft like cheese, so they can be cut with a knife.
- They have low melting points.
- They all react with the oxygen in the air, so they have to be kept under oil.
- Their compounds are similar. The photo shows crystals of sodium chloride (NaCl). Crystals of lithium chloride or potassium chloride would be exactly the same shape.

Transition metals

Mendeleev had a problem finding places for metals like copper, iron and gold in his table. In the modern periodic table these metals form the large central block called the **transition metals**, which is shaded in red in the periodic table on the opposite page.

The transition metals are different from group I metals.

- Most of them are hard and have high melting points (mercury is an exception as it is a liquid at room temperature).
- They react slowly with the oxygen in air.
- The compounds made from transition metals are often coloured. The photo shows iron chloride (left) and copper chloride (right).

d Rubidium (Rb) is a group I element. Give the formula for rubidium chloride.

e Caesium (Cs) is a group I element. Would you leave caesium out in the air? Give reasons for your answer.

f Give three ways in which transition metals are different from group I metals.

Questions

1. What do the following scientific words mean?

   a group   **b** period   **c** element   **d** compound

2. Look at this list of substances.

   iron   water   carbon dioxide   potassium   sodium chloride

   a Which of the substances in the list are compounds?

   b Which of the substances in the list have a place in the periodic table?

   c Explain why some of these substances belong in the periodic table and others do not.

3. The wire used for electric lamp filaments is made of an element called tungsten. Tungsten is hard and has a very high melting point (over 3400 °C).

   a In what ways is tungsten typical of a metallic element?

   b Is tungsten a group I metal or a transition metal? Give reasons for your choice.

When you revise

Each element has a symbol and a place in the periodic table.

The periodic table has periods (rows) and groups (columns). Elements in a group are similar.

Metallic elements are shiny, good electrical and thermal conductors and all are solids at room temperature (except mercury).

Non-metallic elements can be solids, liquids or gases at room temperature and are usually poor electrical and thermal conductors.

4.3 Reactivity of metals

Learn about

♦ Metals reacting

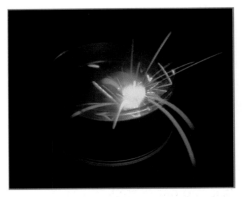

Reactivity

Potassium reacts very quickly, releasing a lot of energy. We say that it is a very **reactive** metal. The photo shows potassium reacting with water. Gold is a very **unreactive** metal. Gold jewellery can last thousands of years without changing, because it does not react with water or oxygen. Potassium has a high **reactivity** and gold has a low reactivity.

Metals reacting with oxygen from the air

Some metals react quickly with the oxygen in the air. Potassium forms a layer of potassium oxide as soon as a newly cut surface is exposed to air. A lump of potassium will burst into flames if left in air. This shows that a lot of energy is released when potassium reacts.

potassium + oxygen → potassium oxide

Magnesium also reacts with the oxygen in the air. Look at the photo opposite. When heated, magnesium burns quickly, releasing energy. However, it releases less energy than potassium, and magnesium can be left out in the air without bursting into flames. Magnesium is less reactive than potassium.

Other metals react more slowly with oxygen in the air, because they are less reactive. Copper reacts slowly, even when heated, forming a layer of copper oxide that dulls the surface. Gold is unreactive. It never reacts with oxygen.

a Which is the least reactive of magnesium, copper and potassium? Give a reason for your choice.

b Write a word equation for the reaction of copper with oxygen.

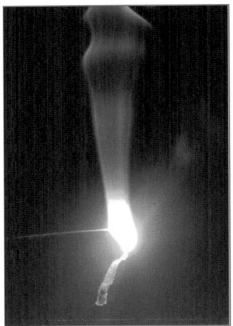

Metals reacting with water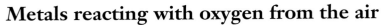

Some very reactive metals, like sodium, react with water. This reaction produces hydrogen and releases a lot of energy.

sodium + water → sodium hydroxide + hydrogen

Calcium also reacts with water, producing calcium hydroxide and hydrogen. Less energy is released than when sodium reacts with water. This means it is safe to do the reaction in a test tube rather than an open container.

calcium + water → calcium hydroxide + hydrogen

Testing for hydrogen
When a lighted splint is put into hydrogen, the hydrogen explodes. This makes a quiet pop.

c Arrange these metals from most reactive to least reactive:

calcium   sodium   gold

d Which of the three metals would release the most energy when it reacted?

Metals reacting with acid

Many metals react with acids, producing hydrogen and a salt. Bubbles of hydrogen are made, and the test tube warms up because of the energy released in the reaction. If sulfuric acid is used, the salt made is a sulfate.

zinc + sulfuric acid → zinc sulfate + hydrogen

When magnesium is reacted with acid, the bubbles of hydrogen are produced more quickly and the test tube gets even hotter. The photo shows zinc (left) and magnesium (right) reacting with hydrochloric acid. Magnesium is more reactive than zinc. If nitric acid is used, the salt made is a nitrate.

magnesium + nitric acid → magnesium nitrate + hydrogen

It is too dangerous to react acid with a very reactive metal like potassium. There would be an explosion because so much energy would be released. If a metal reacts quickly with cold water, then it is far too reactive to put in acid.

Unreactive metals, like copper and gold, do not react with acid.

e Jo puts magnesium, copper and zinc into hydrochloric acid in separate test tubes. She measures the temperature rise for each. Predict her results, giving your reasons.

Questions

1. Malcolm is investigating the reactivity of three metals: potassium, zinc and copper. Malcolm's first idea is to heat a small piece of each material in a Bunsen burner flame.

   a Write a word equation for the reaction that happens when copper is heated in a Bunsen burner flame.

   b Why is Malcolm's plan not safe?

   c Suggest an alternative plan.

2. Compare how potassium, gold and sodium act when you put them in water. Use the information on these pages to help you. Write a word equation for one of the reactions you describe.

3. Loretta is investigating the reactivity of metals by putting them in hydrochloric acid. She would like to include copper, magnesium and potassium in her investigation. Loretta is a Year 9 pupil.

   a Suggest which metal is too dangerous for Loretta to use.

   b Write a word equation for the reaction between magnesium and hydrochloric acid.

   c Predict the outcome of Loretta's experiment if she used copper, magnesium and zinc:

   i Which metals will react?   **ii** Which will react most quickly?

When you revise

Metals react with oxygen to make metal oxides.

Very reactive metals react with water to make hydrogen and a metal hydroxide.

Some metals react with acid to make hydrogen and a salt. The type of salt depends on the type of acid used.

The more reactive the metal, the more energy is released when it reacts.

4.4 Displacement reactions

Metals reacting with metal oxides

If you gently heat zinc and copper oxide they react together, giving out a lot of energy. This is shown in the photo. The reactants burn brightly. When the reaction is finished and has cooled, there is a mixture of brown copper and white zinc oxide.

zinc + copper oxide → zinc oxide + copper

The zinc has pushed the copper out of its compound. The zinc has **displaced** the copper. This is a **displacement reaction**.

Zinc oxide will not react with copper. This is because copper is less reactive than zinc. The more reactive metal pushes the less reactive metal out of the compound.

a Copy and complete this word equation for the displacement reaction between magnesium and copper oxide.

magnesium + copper oxide → _____ _____ + _____

Energy was released in the reaction between copper oxide and zinc. This is because zinc is more reactive than copper.

b Magnesium is a very reactive metal, more reactive than zinc. Which reaction below will release more energy?

  i zinc and copper oxide

  ii magnesium and copper oxide

Winners and losers

The zinc atoms 'want' to be as zinc oxide and the copper atoms 'want' to be as copper oxide. However, there are not enough oxygen atoms to go round, so the atoms of the more reactive metal always win. The zinc atoms end up as zinc oxide and the copper atoms end up as copper.

copper atoms   zinc atoms

oxygen atoms

Displacement reactions in solution

If you mix zinc with copper sulfate solution in a test tube, a chemical reaction occurs and the reactants get hot. After the reaction there are small pieces of solid copper and a colourless solution of zinc sulfate.

zinc + copper sulfate → copper + zinc sulfate

c What sort of reaction happens between zinc and copper sulfate?

The temperature rose because energy was given out during the displacement reaction. The energy heated the water.

d Nickel is less reactive than zinc. Which reaction below will cause a greater rise in temperature?

   i copper sulfate and nickel   **ii** copper sulfate and zinc

Preventing rusting

Iron rusts. When iron rusts it reacts with oxygen to make iron oxide. Rusting can be stopped by putting a more reactive metal such as zinc against the iron. The zinc then reacts with the oxygen instead of the iron. If some iron oxide forms, the zinc will push the iron out, making zinc oxide instead.

e Which is more likely to form a metal oxide, zinc or iron? Give a reason for your answer.

f Write a word equation for the reaction of zinc with iron oxide.

This method of preventing iron rusting is used for ships, submarines and oil rigs. Huge lumps of reactive metal are fixed onto the sides. This reacts with the oxygen instead of the iron. The photo shows lumps of zinc bolted to a boat to protect the steel from rusting.

Questions

1. Magnesium is more reactive than nickel. Nickel sulfate makes a green solution. Magnesium sulfate makes a colourless solution.

  a Write word equations for the following reactions:

    i magnesium and nickel oxide

    ii magnesium and nickel sulfate solution.

  b What would you observe during reaction **ii**?

2. Powdered aluminium will react with iron oxide. The reaction is like the one shown at the top of the opposite page. Melted iron and aluminium oxide are made in the reaction.

  a Which is the more reactive metal, aluminium or iron? Give reasons for your answer.

  b Write a word equation for the reaction.

  c Why is the iron melted, rather than solid?

  d Suggest why the reaction works better with powdered aluminium rather than a lump of aluminium.

When you revise

More reactive metals push less reactive metals out of their compounds. These reactions are called **displacement reactions**.

In a displacement reaction, the more reactive metal ends up in the compound.

Displacement reactions can be useful.

Displacement reactions often release a lot of energy.

4.5 Ranking reactivity

The reactivity series

The **reactivity series** is a list of metals. The most reactive is at the top and the least reactive is at the bottom. Joel is putting ten metals into a reactivity series. The ten metals are calcium (Ca), copper (Cu), gold (Au), iron (Fe), lithium (Li), magnesium (Mg), nickel (Ni), potassium (K), sodium (Na) and zinc (Zn).

First thoughts

The periodic table on the wall of the lab shows photos of all the metals. Joel finds the photos of his ten metals. Sodium and lithium are all stored under oil in the photos. Potassium is sealed in a glass tube. Joel decides that these three metals are probably the most reactive.

a Look at the periodic table on page 46. Which group are lithium, potassium and sodium in?

Reaction with water

Joel finds a video that shows lithium, potassium and sodium reacting with cold water. All three react, and all three reactions make hydrogen. However, lithium reacts the slowest and potassium reacts the fastest, with sodium in between. He writes them in order of reactivity:

potassium
sodium
lithium

Joel then decides to check the reactivity of all the metals with cold water. He finds out that he cannot include potassium and sodium in his experiment, because they are too dangerous. However, he can use a very small piece of lithium if the teacher watches carefully. He has to do the reaction in a beaker, not a test tube. Joel puts a bit of each metal into cold water in a small beaker. The table shows his results.

Metal	Observation
Calcium	Many bubbles, made quickly
Copper	No reaction
Gold	No reaction
Iron	No reaction
Lithium	Most bubbles, made very quickly
Magnesium	A few bubbles, made very slowly
Nickel	No reaction
Zinc	No reaction

b Which metals reacted with water in Joel's experiment?

c Put these metals in order of reactivity, with the most reactive at the top.

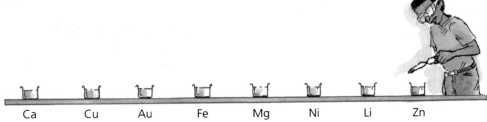

Ca Cu Au Fe Mg Ni Li Zn

Reaction with dilute acid

Joel decides to react the metals with hydrochloric acid. His teacher tells him that calcium and lithium are far too reactive to put in acid. Joel tests copper, gold, iron, magnesium, nickel and zinc with hydrochloric acid. He was surprised to find that only magnesium and zinc reacted and magnesium made many more bubbles and more quickly.

Joel can now write a reactivity series for six of the metals like this:

potassium
sodium
lithium
calcium
magnesium
zinc

Displacement reactions

Joel is still not sure of the order of the last four: copper (Cu), gold (Au), iron (Fe) and nickel (Ni).

He decides to use displacement reactions to sort out the last four metals.

For his experiment he uses copper sulfate, iron sulfate and nickel sulfate. Joel records the experiment in the table below. If there is a colour change, then a reaction happened. No colour change means no reaction. Joel ticked the combinations that had reacted.

		Metal		
		Nickel	Copper	Iron
	Nickel sulfate		Before After	Before After ✓
Metal compound	Copper sulfate	Before After ✓		Before After ✓
	Iron sulfate	Before After	Before After	

d **Which metal pushed nickel out of the nickel sulfate?**

e **Which metals pushed copper out of the copper sulfate?**

f **Out of copper, iron and nickel which is:**

   i   the most reactive metal?

   ii   the least reactive metal?

Joel tries putting some gold metal with each of the sulfate solutions. The gold does not push any of the other metals from their compounds. This shows that gold is the least reactive metal.

g   Write a reactivity series for all ten metals.

Questions

1. Joel reacted lithium with water in one of his experiments.
   a   Why was Joel only allowed to use a very small piece of lithium?
   b   Why was it safer to use a small beaker rather than a test tube when reacting lithium with water?
   c   What other safety precautions would Joel have taken when doing the experiments?

2. Bimla put some copper coins in silver nitrate solution. After some time, the coins went silvery, and the solution started to have a slight green-blue colour.
   a   Is silver below or above copper in the reactivity series? Give reasons for your answer.
   b   When ancient jewellery is dug up, silver items are badly corroded but gold ones look 'as new'. Is silver above or below gold in the reactivity series?
   c   Would a gold coin become coated with silver when placed in silver nitrate solution? Give a reason for your answer.

When you revise

The **reactivity series** is a list of metals with the most reactive at the top and the least reactive at the bottom.

4.6 Working together

Rusting away

Iron corrodes. The iron is changed into iron oxide, or rust. The rust crumbles away. The rusting reaction needs oxygen and water. It is speeded up by salt. Rusting is prevented if there is a more reactive metal in contact with the iron. The more reactive metal corrodes instead of the iron. The variables that affect rusting include:

1 iron   **2** oxygen   **3** water   **4** time   **5** salt
6 a more reactive metal in contact with the iron   **7** temperature.

a For each variable in the list above, use one of the sentence endings below to write a complete sentence.

… is needed for rusting to happen.

… increases the amount of rusting.

… decreases the amount of rusting.

Iron is used to make cars, bridges, the skeletons of buildings, ships, nails and screws, steel cables, pans, radiators, bicycles and thousands of other items. Stopping rusting saves billions of pounds.

b Explain how each of the following prevents rusting.

i painting   **ii** oiling

iii keeping the object indoors

iv making the object of aluminium

v washing the underside of a car after winter

vi lumps of reactive metal in contact with iron

Digesting proteins

In digestion large, insoluble molecules are broken down into small, soluble molecules. Jezzie was investigating the digestion of egg white protein. She found out these facts about the digestion of proteins.

♦ It happens in the stomach.

♦ There is an enzyme called pepsin in the stomach that breaks down proteins.

♦ The stomach is acidic, about pH 2, and at 37 °C, which is body temperature.

♦ The food is chewed and churned to speed up digestion.

♦ Digestion in the stomach takes about 20 minutes.

Jezzie made this list of the variables that may affect digestion.

♦ pepsin (the enzyme)   ♦ pH   ♦ temperature
♦ surface area of the protein   ♦ time

Jezzie decided to investigate pH and temperature. The protein she used was cooked egg white. Digestion is finished when the white, opaque protein turns colourless and transparent. Jezzie planned a fair test using the same amount of enzyme and the same surface area for the protein. She checked the tubes after 6 hours. The following table shows her results.

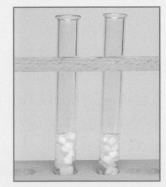

Before digestion.

After digestion.

Temperature in °C								
pH	15	25	35	45	55	65	75	85
0	✗	✔	✔	✔	✗	✗	✔	✔
1	✗	✔	✔	✔	✗	✗	✗	✗
2	✗	✔	✔	✔	✗	✗	✗	✗
3	✗	✗	✔	✗	✗	✗	✗	✗
4	✗	✗	✗	✗	✗	✗	✗	✗

✔✔ = digestion finished at 6 hours   ✗ = digestion not finished at 6 hours

Jezzie noticed that there were two groups of test tubes in which digestion happened – the group marked by red ticks and the group marked by blue ticks. Jezzie's teacher suggested that she repeat the experiment without the pepsin present. Here are her results.

Temperature in °C								
pH	15	25	35	45	55	65	75	85
0	✗	✗	✗	✗	✗	✗	✔	✔
1	✗	✗	✗	✗	✗	✗	✗	✗
2	✗	✗	✗	✗	✗	✗	✗	✗
3	✗	✗	✗	✗	✗	✗	✗	✗
4	✗	✗	✗	✗	✗	✗	✗	✗

✔ = digestion finished at 6 hours   ✗ = digestion not finished at 6 hours

c In how many test tubes had digestion finished at 6 hours?

d Why did Jezzie's teacher suggest repeating the experiment without pepsin?

e At what temperature and pH does digestion happen without pepsin?

f Compare the two results tables. At what temperature and pH does digestion happen with pepsin?

g Suggest what is needed for digestion to happen in the stomach. Give your reasons.

h Write a conclusion for Jezzie's investigation.

Questions

1. Under which of the following conditions will pepsin digest proteins the quickest? Give your reasons.

   a pH 2 and 35 °C   **b** pH 1 and 55 °C   **c** pH 3 and 25 °C

2. Jezzie goes on to investigate surface area. She changes how much she chops up the egg white. She wants to look at digestion by pepsin, because this is what happens in the stomach.

   a What temperature should Jezzie choose? Give your reasons.

   b What pH should Jezzie choose? Give your reasons.

   c Predict the effect of increasing the surface area on the amount of digestion in 6 hours. Give reasons for your prediction.

3. Imagine that you are a scientist working for a company making bolts that are used to build bridges and buildings. Your job is to test all the new bolts to see how rustproof they are. Rusting is a slow process, so you need to set up conditions which will make the bolts rust as quickly as possible. Design a 'rusting box' for maximum rusting.

5.1 Great medical breakthroughs

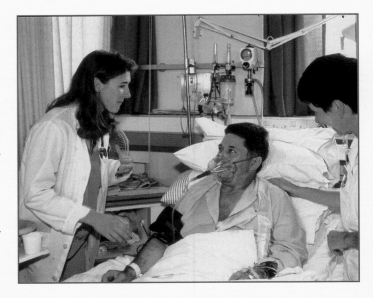

Treating and preventing disease

Over 2000 years ago, people in the Middle East used over 200 different plants to treat illnesses. The Greeks also used many different plants. The famous Greek doctor Hippocrates used willow bark to help patients in pain. The bark contains a chemical which we use today, called aspirin.

Over the past 400 years many medical discoveries have been made. Because of these we are now able to cure or prevent many diseases which used to kill people. Read about some of these discoveries below.

In 1867, Joseph Lister, an English doctor, discovered carbolic acid. This was the first widely used antiseptic. It made operations safer because it stopped wounds becoming infected.

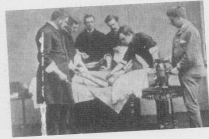

Using a carbolic acid spray during an operation.

Alexander Fleming made one of the greatest medical breakthroughs by chance in 1928. Fleming was growing bacteria on a special dish. He noticed that some mould had got onto a dish and it was stopping the bacteria growing. He grew more of the mould and obtained a substance from it called penicillin. He found it could destroy a number of different bacteria. In 1941, Howard Florey and Ernst Chain found a way of making penicillin in large amounts to use as a medicine.

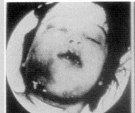

The first child to be treated with penicillin. Four weeks after treatment the infection was gone.

In 1796, the English doctor Edward Jenner performed the first vaccination against smallpox. Jenner had noticed that milkmaids did not get smallpox, but got a milder form of the disease called cowpox. Jenner took the pus from cowpox spots on a sterile needle and scratched it into the skin of a boy called James Phipps. James developed cowpox, but he did not develop smallpox. He was protected against smallpox.

Edward Jenner.

a What is special about the bark of the willow tree?

b Why was James Phipps important?

c What is an antiseptic used for?

How the human body functions

The study of medicine, or being a doctor, is more than just treating patients with drugs. It is also about understanding how the human body works. Our knowledge of the human body has improved a great deal over the last 500 years. Scientists who study the human body are called **physiologists**.

Andreas Vesalius was born in Brussels in 1514. He gave the first full description of the human body in his book *Concerning the Fabric of the Human Body* in 1543.

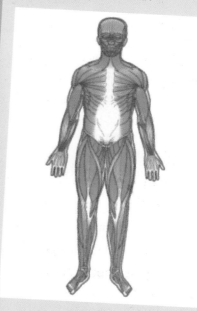

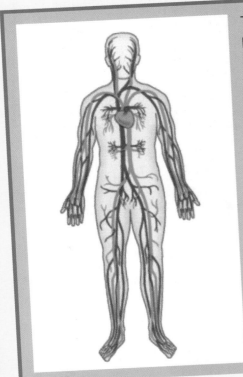

The English doctor William Harvey published a full account of how the blood circulates around the body in 1628. He even suggested that capillaries existed, although he could not see them.

Claude Bernard was a nineteenth-century French physiologist. He discovered that glucose was the main source of energy for the body. He also found that the glucose was stored in the liver.

The discoveries above are some of the main highlights of medicine in previous centuries. During the last century, there were too many new discoveries to mention them all.

d What is the name of the process in the body that releases energy from glucose?

e Which important medical discovery from the last century would you add to the list?

Questions

1. Write the names of the scientists along with the discovery each one made.

Scientists	Discoveries
Alexander Fleming	full account of how the blood circulates
Joseph Lister	first widely used antiseptic
William Harvey	vaccination for smallpox
Edward Jenner	the first antibiotic

2. Discuss the idea that many medical discoveries have happened by chance. Do you agree with this idea?

3. Why do you think there were so many more medical discoveries in the twentieth century than there had been before?

4. Make a time line of all the medical breakthroughs mentioned on these pages.

5.2 Keeping fit

What is fitness?

You don't have to decide how to breathe, it happens automatically. Your brain changes how quickly you breathe, or your **breathing rate**, without you having to think about it.

Exercising

When you exercise, your muscle cells need to carry out more respiration to release energy. They need more oxygen and they also produce more carbon dioxide, so your breathing rate is faster.

At rest, your body needs energy only for the life processes that keep the body functioning. Your cells need less oxygen so your breathing rate slows down. The graph shows how the breathing rate may change during the day for two different people.

(a) Why do you think the breathing rate is low between midnight and 6 a.m. for both people?

(b) Why do you think that the breathing rate goes up and down during the day?

(c) Why do you think the two lines on the graph are different?

Unfit people get out of breath easily. But being fit is about more than just how you breathe.

Respiration

When you breathe in, you take in oxygen to be used in respiration. Respiration is the process in which glucose and oxygen react to release energy from our food. The products are carbon dioxide and water vapour. As you breathe out the body gets rid of these two waste gases.

oxygen + glucose → water + carbon dioxide

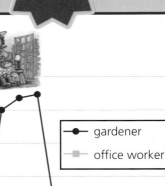

energy is released

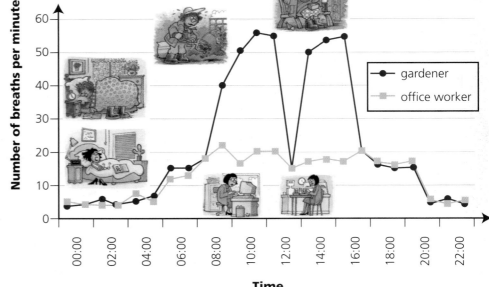

Measuring your fitness

One of the easiest ways to measure your fitness is to see how quickly your heart is beating. You measure your pulse rate to tell you this. In a fit person, the heart pumps more efficiently because it has grown larger with regular exercise. This means:

♦ Your resting pulse rate is quite low.

♦ During exercise, your pulse rate does not increase too much.

♦ After exercise, your pulse rate quickly returns to normal.

In unfit people, the pulse rate is higher. When they exercise, the pulse rate increases quite a lot. It takes a long time for their pulse rate to return to normal.

Keeping fit and healthy

Doctors say that we should exercise regularly about three times a week to stay healthy. Exercise helps to keep your heart healthy and prevent heart disease. It also keeps the lungs and the rest of your body fit.

Regular exercise keeps your body working properly. It improves the circulation of the blood and builds strong muscles. It can make your lungs bigger so you breathe more efficiently. It helps keep your weight at a healthy level. Regular exercise also keeps your bones and joints working well.

As well as taking regular exercise, we should also make sure that we eat a balanced diet. Food provides us with energy and allows our bodies to grow and repair themselves. We need to make sure we don't over-eat or under-eat. Both are bad for our health. To be healthy we should avoid drugs such as nicotine and alcohol. It is also important to get enough rest and sleep.

d Why do you think exercise keeps your body healthy?

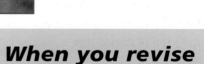

Questions

1. Explain what happens when you exercise using the following words:
   pulse rate   carbon dioxide   breathing rate   oxygen

2. **a** Make a list of all the things we need to do to keep healthy.

   b Make a list of all the parts of your body that benefit from a healthy lifestyle.

3. Make a chart of all the activities you do in a day. Put the activities in order to show which ones you think use the most energy, and say how they keep you fit.

4. Design a brochure for a sports centre describing to people why they need to stay fit and use the sports centre more often.

When you revise

The **breathing rate** increases during exercise to supply the muscle cells with the oxygen they need for respiration.

Regular exercise is good for your muscles, your lungs, your circulation, your bones and your joints.

A healthy lifestyle includes a good balanced diet, keeping the right weight, taking enough rest and avoiding drugs.

5.3 Breathe in and out

How do your lungs work?

If you put your hands on your chest, you can feel it move up and down as you breathe in and out. Your lungs are in your chest. The oxygen you need for respiration gets into your body through your lungs, and the waste carbon dioxide is removed from your body through your lungs.

a Write a word equation for respiration.

The lungs are organs. Like all organs, the lungs are made of different types of tissue. Each tissue is made up of similar specialised cells. The lungs, together with the tubes that take gases in and out of the lungs, form an organ system.

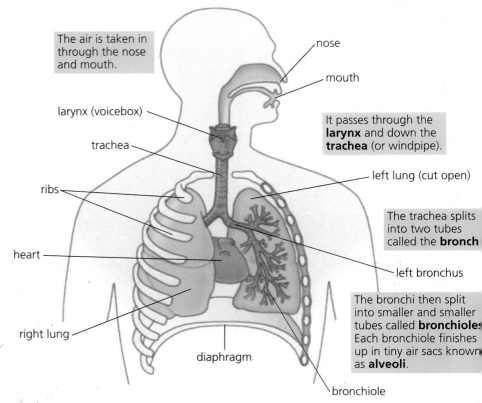

The air is taken in through the nose and mouth.

nose

mouth

larynx (voicebox)

trachea

ribs

heart

right lung

diaphragm

It passes through the **larynx** and down the **trachea** (or windpipe).

left lung (cut open)

The trachea splits into two tubes called the **bronch**

left bronchus

The bronchi then split into smaller and smaller tubes called **bronchiole** Each bronchiole finishes up in tiny air sacs known as **alveoli**.

bronchiole

Oxygen in, carbon dioxide out

The bar chart shows how much oxygen and carbon dioxide there is in the air you breathe in and the air you breathe out.

b Which gas is there more of in the air you breathe out than in the air you breathe in?

c Which gas in the air you breathe in is used up in the body?

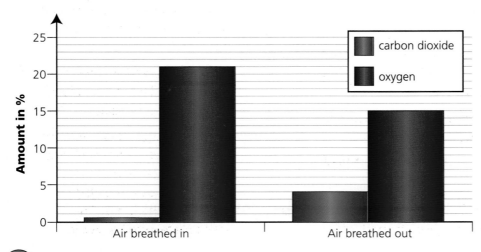

You have tiny air sacs in your lungs called **alveoli**. The diagram shows what happens in the alveoli. The walls of the alveoli are very thin. Gases can move very easily through the thin walls of the alveoli. There are many capillaries carrying blood near the alveoli.

The oxygen molecules in the lungs move through the walls of the alveoli into the blood in the capillaries. At the same time, carbon dioxide molecules move in the opposite direction, from the blood in the capillaries into the alveoli. The movement of oxygen into the blood and carbon dioxide out of the blood is called **gas exchange**.

Capillaries are very narrow tubes with very thin walls. This means that all the blood inside is very close to the capillary walls so oxygen and carbon dioxide can move through.

d Which gas moves from the blood into the air in the alveoli?

The blood in the capillaries carries oxygen to all the cells in the body, and carbon dioxide away from them. The blood carries the carbon dioxide back to the alveoli so it can be removed from the body by the lungs.

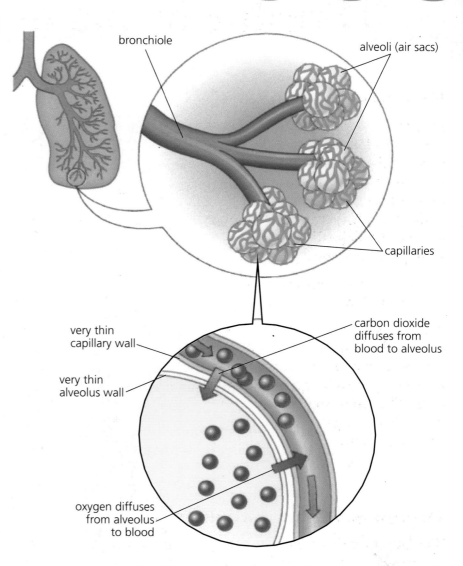

Questions

1. Copy and complete these sentences.

   The _____ are small air sacs that have very _____ walls. Oxygen moves through the walls of the alveoli and ends up in the _____. At the same time, _____ _____ moves from the capillaries into the alveoli. We call this process gas _____.

2. Compare the air you breathe in with the air you breathe out. Explain how it is different, and why.

3. Why can the gas particles move easily between the blood and the alveoli?

4. You are an oxygen molecule. Describe your journey from the air into the blood. Name all the parts you pass through.

When you revise

Oxygen is needed for respiration, and carbon dioxide is a waste product.

The air we breathe in has more oxygen and less carbon dioxide than the air we breathe out.

Gas exchange happens when oxygen moves from the lungs into the blood and carbon dioxide moves out of the blood into the lungs. This takes place in the **alveoli**.

5.4 Smoking and drinking

Smoking

It has been known since the 1960s that smoking is bad for our health, but about a third of people in the UK smoke. Many smokers die of illnesses caused by or made worse by smoking. Someone dies every 10 minutes as a direct result of smoking.

Why is smoking bad for you?

We know the effect on the body of the three main substances in cigarettes: nicotine, tar and carbon monoxide.

> **Carbon monoxide** is a poisonous gas that stops your red blood cells carrying oxygen.

> **Nicotine** is the drug in cigarettes that makes you feel good if you smoke. When the effect wears off, you want more nicotine again. This is called **addiction**. Once you are addicted to a drug, it is very difficult to stop using it. Nicotine affects your brain, nervous system and circulatory system. It can cause heart disease.

> **Tar** is a mixture of chemicals that collects in your lungs. It clogs up the alveoli. This makes the lungs less able to take in all the oxygen the body needs, and makes many smokers cough. Some of the chemicals in tar cause cancer of the lungs.

Other diseases caused by smoking include cancer of the throat and mouth, bronchitis, heart disease and problems with the circulatory system.

Passive smoking

When people smoke cigarettes, most of the smoke goes into their lungs. Some of it also goes into the air around them, which others breathe in. This is called **passive smoking**. The children of smokers are more likely to suffer from lung diseases such as pneumonia and bronchitis because of passive smoking.

ⓐ What are the main chemicals in cigarette smoke?

ⓑ Describe how smoking can damage your lungs.

A healthy lung.   *The lung of a smoker.*

Drinking

Alcohol (or ethanol) is found in beer, wine and spirits. It is easily available and many people enjoy a drink now and then. But alcohol can have long-term effects if people drink too much and become addicted to it.

To begin with, a drink makes you feel relaxed. More alcohol slows your reactions and affects your co-ordination and balance. A lot of alcohol makes you speak slowly and not very clearly. You may vomit and become unconscious. Alcohol affects people differently. The effect depends on their weight, sex, age and how much they have eaten.

How much alcohol?

Alcohol is measured in **units**. All of the drinks in the diagram contain one unit of alcohol.

After drinking three units of alcohol, your reactions become too slow to drive. This is why it is illegal to drive after drinking more than three units. If you are driving, it is safest not to drink any alcohol at all. Every year, in Britain, around 3500 people are killed or seriously injured in accidents with drivers who have been drinking.

| ½ pint of beer | single measure of spirits | small glass of wine | small glass of sherry | all = 1 unit of alcohol |

Getting rid of the alcohol

Alcohol is removed from the blood by the liver. The liver can remove one unit of alcohol per hour. If a person has drunk 6 units of alcohol, it will take 6 hours before the blood returns to normal.

People who drink too much are likely to suffer from a variety of illnesses, including a damaged liver, cancer and brain damage.

Government campaigns

Every Christmas the Government warns against the dangers of drinking and driving. There are warnings on every packet of cigarettes, and the manufacturers have to tell us how much tar the cigarettes contain. Tobacco firms are not allowed to advertise on television.

c Stephen drinks two pints of beer and a measure of whiskey. How many units of alcohol has he drunk?

d How long would it take the liver to remove the following amounts of alcohol?

  i 3 units

  ii 4 glasses of wine

  iii 4 pints of lager

More than **400** people will be killed this year as a result of drink driving

DON'T DRINK AND DRIVE

Questions

1. Write each word along with its meaning.

Words	Meanings
nicotine	a disease of the lungs
carbon monoxide	an addictive chemical that can cause heart disease
bronchitis	a mixture of chemicals that collects in the lungs
tar	a poisonous gas

2. Explain why it is dangerous to drink alcohol before driving a car or before swimming.

3. Design a poster to help educate teenagers about the dangers of smoking.

4. In a group, discuss the following statements. Explain why you think each idea is a good one or a bad one for reducing the problems due to alcohol.

   a The age at which you are allowed to buy alcohol should be raised from 18 to 21.

   b The legal limit for driving should be reduced to 1 unit.

   c The price of alcoholic drinks should be increased.

When you revise

Cigarette smoke contains **nicotine**, **tar** and **carbon monoxide**. Tar harms the lungs.

Nicotine and **alcohol** are both **addictive** drugs which can have a harmful effect on the body.

63

5.5 Going on growing

Marvellous microorganisms

A microorganism is a living thing that is so small it can only be seen clearly with a microscope. Microorganisms are sometimes called **microbes**. Many of them are only a fraction of a millimetre long. To describe their size, scientists use a unit called the **micrometre** (μm).

$$1\,\mu m = \frac{1}{1000}\,mm = \frac{1}{10\,000}\,cm = \frac{1}{1\,000\,000}\,m$$

Types of microbe

There are very many different microbes, but there are three main types:

Bacteria are very small, usually about 1 μm across. A bacterium is a single-celled organism. They have a cell wall, but do not have a nucleus.

Viruses are much smaller than bacteria. They are not made of cells. They have a coat made from protein, and inside is a piece of DNA.

coat
DNA

a Give one way in which bacteria are similar to plant cells.

b Give one way in which bacteria are different from plant cells.

Some **fungi**, such as yeast, are small and round. Others, like mould, are made of long threads called **hyphae**. These threads can only be seen clearly under a microscope.

hyphae

Cell division

To grow well, microbes need to be kept warm and moist and have plenty of food. A microbe such as yeast feeds on sugar.

Yeast reproduces by one cell dividing to make two cells, as shown in the photo. This is called **cell division**. The two cells grow a little bigger and then they also divide in two. In this way a population of yeast starts off by growing slowly, but then grows very rapidly.

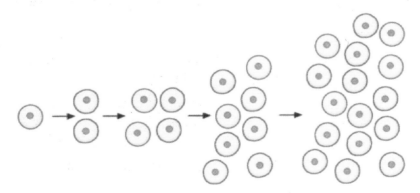

1 cell → 2 cells → 4 cells → 8 cells → 16 cells …

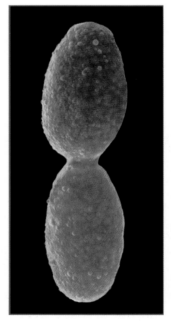

c Look at the sequence of cell numbers opposite. Give the next five steps in the sequence.

The number of yeast cells doubles with every division. If the conditions are right, then the yeast would continue to grow like this. But as the population gets bigger and bigger it begins to grow more slowly as the yeast cells have to compete for food and space.

Some bacteria can divide every 20 minutes. This means that in just one day there could be 4 722 366 482 869 650 000 000 offspring from just one bacterium!

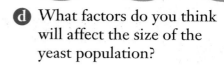

d What factors do you think will affect the size of the yeast population?

Humans and growth

Human bodies grow because our cells divide in the same way as bacteria and fungi. We started life as a single fertilised egg cell that divided to produce a human baby. Even when we become adults our cells are still dividing. Old cells are constantly being replaced by new ones. New skin cells and blood cells are needed to repair the body.

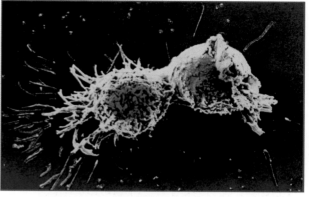

New blood cells are made by cell division.

Useful microbes

Some microbes are very useful to us. The table shows some of the ways that we use them.

Type of microbe	Uses
Fungi	Yeast is used to produce beer and wine. Yeast is used to make bread rise when it is baked. Fungi are used in making medicines such as antibiotics. Mould is used in making blue cheese. Fungi decompose dead plants and animals and their waste. Fungi called Quorn can be eaten.
Bacteria	Bacteria are used in making yoghurt and cheese. Bacteria are also used in making medicines. Bacteria decompose dead plants and animals and their waste. Bacteria are used in sewage farms to break down sewage. Some bacteria live inside humans' and other animals' intestines and help to digest their food.

Questions

1. Give three differences between viruses and bacteria.

2. Explain why cell division is important for us to grow.

3. Some yeast cells were put in a closed container with some sugar and water and kept warm. What do you think happened to the population of yeast cells? Explain your answer.

4. The 'Rights for Microbes' campaign manager has asked for your help. Produce a poster to give a positive image of microbes to the public and explain how useful they are.

5. Imagine that scientists have discovered a way to kill every single type of microbe on the planet. Write a story about how this would have a serious effect on our lives.

When you revise

There are three main groups of **microbe**: bacteria, viruses and **fungi**.

Bacteria and fungi reproduce by **cell division**.

Cell division makes it possible for humans to grow and repair their bodies.

Microorganisms can be very useful to us.

5.6 Defence against disease

Disease

The air around you is full of microbes. Your body is covered in them. Many microbes are harmless, but some can cause **infections** or diseases if they get inside our bodies. Organisms that cause disease are called **pathogens**.

The table shows some diseases caused by the different types of microbe. The photos show tuberculosis (**A**), chickenpox (**B**) and athlete's foot (**C**).

Bacteria	Viruses	Fungi
Meningitis (bacterial)	Meningitis (viral)	Athlete's foot
Food poisoning	Cold	Ringworm
Whooping cough	Influenza ('flu)	
Tetanus	Chickenpox	
Tuberculosis (TB)	German measles	
	Rabies	
	AIDS	

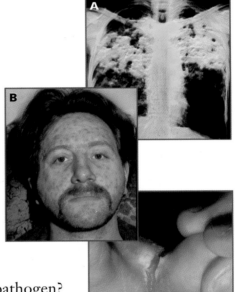

The yellow parts of the lungs have been damaged by TB.

a What is a pathogen?

How microbes enter the body

The human body is very good at keeping microbes out. The skin is a good barrier and stops microbes from getting into the blood. Tears contain a chemical that destroys bacteria. But there are several ways that microbes can get past these defences and enter the body.

b List two ways in which your body keeps bacteria out.

Cuts in the skin allow microbes in.

The water you drink can carry microbes.

Sexually transmitted diseases such as AIDS can be caught from sexual intercourse without protection.

The food you eat can contain harmful microbes.

Air has lots of microbes in it, which you can breathe in.

Animals can carry diseases and pass them on by biting you.

Fighting infection

Once microbes get inside the body, there is still another line of defence in the blood which can attack them. This is called the **immune system**. **White blood cells** help in the fight against microbes and are a vital part of the immune system. They work in three different ways.

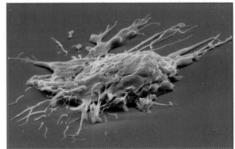

A white blood cell swallowing up bacteria (pink rods).

1. Some white blood cells can swallow up microbes.

2. White blood cells produce special chemicals called **antibodies** which attach themselves to the outside of the microbes. Antibodies may kill the microbes directly, or they may make them clump together, which makes it easier for white blood cells to swallow them up.

3. White blood cells can destroy the toxic chemicals produced by microbes.

Immunisation

An antibody is only able to recognise and fight one type of microbe. Once your immune system has met a microbe, the antibodies can be made quite easily and the body can fight the infection a lot quicker. This makes you **immune** to the disease.

You can be **vaccinated** to make you immune to a disease before you catch it. Dead or inactive microbes can be injected into your body. They do not make you ill, but your body will produce antibodies against them.

Antibodies can be passed from a mother to her baby across the placenta and also in breast milk. New babies are protected by these antibodies.

c **i** What is an antibody?
    ii How does it fight infection?

Vaccinations control diseases

Rubella (German measles) is a mild disease that gives you a slight rash. But if a pregnant woman catches rubella, the infection may spread to the embryo and leave the baby blind, deaf or possibly brain damaged. It is important that girls are vaccinated against rubella so that they and their babies are protected against the disease. Many people have vaccinations before they go on holiday.

Questions

1. Explain how the following situations can spread disease:
   a not washing your hands after going to the toilet
   b sneezing in someone's face
   c drug users sharing syringes.

2. Survey your class to find out who has had chickenpox, measles, mumps, colds and 'flu. Find out how many times each person has had each disease. For each disease:
   a How many people have had the disease once?
   b How many have had the disease more than once?
   c What does this tell you about this disease?

3. **a** What is a vaccine?
   b How does it work?

When you revise

Microorganisms that cause **infection** are called **pathogens**.

The first line of defence in the body is the skin.

The **immune system** can fight off infection using **white blood cells** and **antibodies**.

The immune system can be helped by **vaccinations**.

67

5.7 Medicines and drugs

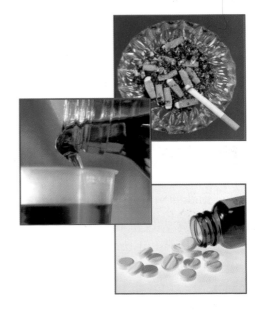

What is a drug?

A **drug** is any substance that is taken into your body and affects the way that you think or feel. Nicotine and alcohol are examples of drugs. It is legal to take some drugs, such as nicotine and alcohol. Society allows adults to use these drugs. Coffee and tea contain a legal drug called caffeine. Many drugs are addictive.

A **medicine** is a drug that if used correctly can make your body work properly or get better. Medicines are usually prescribed by a doctor. Medicines can cause serious problems if you use too much, or if you take them when you are not ill.

a What is the meaning of the word 'drug'?

b What is the difference between a drug and a medicine?

Antibiotics

Antibiotics are very commonly used drugs that can kill some types of bacteria. Penicillin is an antibiotic. Antibiotics only work against bacteria. They will not kill viruses. This is why your doctor may give you an antibiotic for a sore throat, but not for chickenpox.

c Which of these diseases should be treated with antibiotics?

**whooping cough   German measles   a cold
'flu   rabies   tetanus**

Illegal drugs

Many drugs are **illegal**, which means it is against the law to use them. They can all have harmful effects on the body, and most of them are addictive. They are grouped according to the effect they have on the body.

Some solvents in glue, paints and lighter fluid can be breathed in through the nose and mouth. This is called **solvent abuse**. It can make you act strangely and harm yourself and others. It can damage your brain, kidneys and liver.

Depressants such as heroin slow down your body's reactions and make you feel drowsy and relaxed. They can cause mental problems and even death by stopping you breathing. Alcohol is a legal depressant drug.

Stimulants such as cocaine speed up your body's reactions and make you feel as if you have lots of energy. They can cause heart failure. Legal stimulants include caffeine in coffee and nicotine in cigarette smoke.

Hallucinogens such as LSD, ecstasy and cannabis affect the brain. They make you sense things that are not really there. These **hallucinations** can make you behave in ways that may harm yourself or others. Drugs such as LSD and ecstasy can lead to mental illness and brain damage.

d Which type of drug do you think seems to have the most harmful effects?

Drugs and the law

The law divides illegal drugs into three classes. The punishment for having these drugs or trying to sell them to others is shown in the table.

Class of drug	Example of drug	Maximum penalties
Class A	Cocaine Ecstasy Heroin LSD Magic mushrooms	**Having the drug** 7 years in prison and/or a fine **Trying to sell the drug** life imprisonment and/or a fine
Class B	Cannabis	**Having the drug** 5 years in prison and/or a fine **Trying to sell the drug** 14 years in prison and/or a fine
Class C	Valium Steroids	**Having the drug** 2 years in prison and/or a fine **Trying to sell the drug** 5 years in prison and/or a fine

e The punishment for having an illegal drug is not as bad as the punishment for selling it. Why do you think this is?

Questions

1. Copy and complete these sentences.

   A _____ is a substance that affects your body. Some drugs are_____ which means it is against the law to take them. Drugs such as heroin slow your body down and are called _____. Other drugs speed your body up and are called _____. Some drugs make you see things that are not there. We say they give you _____.

2. Name three legal drugs and three illegal drugs.

3. The Government often has campaigns to stop people smoking or drinking. Do you think it would be better to make cigarettes and alcohol illegal? Explain your reasons.

4. Explain what is meant by addiction.

5. Produce an information leaflet for a doctor's waiting room that warns young people of the dangers of drugs.

When you revise

A **drug** is any substance that is taken into the body and affects the way that you think or feel.

Medicines are drugs designed to fight disease or make the body work better.

Drugs, including alcohol and nicotine, can have serious effects on the body and brain and may be addictive.

Testing medicines

A new medicine

How do scientists design new medicines? They start by looking at what causes a disease and how it affects the body. This gives them clues about which chemicals might help to treat the disease.

New medicines are first tested on animals and then on human volunteers to make sure they are safe. Only then can medicines be given by doctors to any patient that needs them.

a Why do you think so much testing is needed before the drugs are used on patients?

Correlation

The scientists need to see if the medicine is going to make patients get better. They want to see if there is a link, or a **correlation**, between a patient taking the medicine and getting better. No correlation means there is no link – the medicine does not make the patient get better.

Scientists divide the patients into two groups. One group is given the new medicine, and the other group is given a **placebo**. A placebo acts as a control – it does not contain any medicine at all.

There are three types of correlation:

◆ If the medicine works then there is a positive correlation.

◆ If the medicine does not work then there is a negative correlation.

◆ If the numbers of people getting better and not getting better are the same then there is no correlation.

b Why do you think the control patients are given a placebo instead of being given no treatment at all?

A new drug

Dr Franklin was testing a new drug for arthritis. She tested 40 patients. Half were given drug B182 and the other half were given a placebo. Out of the 20 patients given drug B182, 15 showed a positive effect (an improvement) and 5 showed no effect. Out of the 20 patients given the placebo, 1 patient showed a positive effect and 19 showed no effect.

To see if there is a correlation between taking drug B182 and an improvement in the arthritis, we use a table like this one:

The 15 people in box **A** and the 19 people in box **D** proved that the new drug worked.

To find out what the correlation is in the results, we calculate the ratio between **A + D** and **C + B**:

$$A + D : C + B = (15 + 19) : (5 + 1)$$
$$= 34 : 6$$

If **A + D** is higher than **B + C** then there is a positive correlation. If **A + D** is lower than **B + C** then there is a negative correlation. If the numbers are the same then there is no correlation.

e What type of correlation can you see in the example above?

f What does this test tell you about drug B182?

	Treated	Not treated
Positive effect	**A** 15	**B** 1
No effect	**C** 5	**D** 19

c Why do the 19 people in box **D** suggest the drug worked?

d How many people's results suggested the drug didn't work?

More tests for reliability

Dr Franklin then set up another experiment for drug B182 in another part of the country. She did this to check how reliable her results were. She gave 20 people drug B182 and another 20 people took a placebo.

Here are the results:
Out of the 20 people using drug B182, 2 showed signs of improvement and 18 did not.
Out of the 20 people not using the drug, 18 showed signs of improvement and 2 did not.

	Treated	Not treated
Positive effect	**A**	**B**
No effect	**C**	**D**

g Copy and complete this table using the results above.

h Calculate the ratio **A + D : B + C**.

i What type of correlation does this show?

j What does this set of results tell you about drug B182?

Questions

1. Why do you think Dr Franklin repeated her experiment in another part of the country?

2. Do you think the sample size in the trial was big enough? Give your reasons.

3. What do you think Dr Franklin's team should do next?

4. Look at the table opposite. For each of these drugs say what type of correlation there is. Show all of your working out.

Drug	Drug given, positive effect	No drug, positive effect	Drug given, no effect	No drug, no effect
U	3	17	19	1
V	10	10	10	10
W	14	3	6	17
X	11	8	9	12

6.1 Hot and cold

Measuring temperature

We decide how hot something is by measuring its **temperature**. We use the **Celsius scale**, which has freezing water at 0° and boiling water at 100°. We show that a temperature is being measured on the Celsius scale by putting °C after it. The Celsius scale for temperature was created by Anders Celsius in 1742.

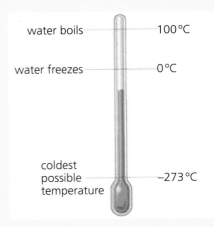

water boils — 100 °C

water freezes — 0 °C

coldest possible temperature — −273 °C

a Suggest three things that have a temperature above 100 °C.

b Suggest three things that have a temperature below 0 °C.

How cold is cold?

The coldest part of the Earth is near the poles in midwinter. One of the coldest days ever recorded was at Vostok in Antarctica, where the temperature fell to −89 °C. However, scientists have measured temperatures much colder than −89 °C, using powerful refrigerators to cool things down.

When nitrogen is cooled it condenses and becomes a liquid. This happens at −196 °C. The photo shows liquid nitrogen. It is boiling, because it has been taken out of the powerful freezer and is heating up. Water vapour from the air has condensed and frozen on the flask, because it is so cold.

c Look at the photo of liquid nitrogen. What in the photo is:

   i heating up?   **ii** cooling down?

The coldest place in the Solar System is Triton, a moon that orbits Neptune. The average temperature on Triton is −235 °C. The lowest temperature you can get is −273 °C.

If something is very cold, it has very little energy. A cup of hot coffee has lots of energy. The particles in the solution are moving quickly, sliding over each other. When the coffee cools the particles move more slowly. If you froze the coffee, the particles would only vibrate on the spot, no longer changing places. Energy has been transferred away from the particles in the coffee as the coffee cooled. If you kept cooling the coffee, the particles would finally stop moving. The coffee would end up at −273 °C.

Triton is the coldest place in the Solar System.

d Copy and complete this sentence, using your knowledge about energy.

   The particles in the hot coffee have lots of _____ energy. This is transferred away from the particles as _____ energy to the air as the coffee cools.

Heating up

One of the hottest places on Earth is Death Valley in California. In the summer of 1917 there were 43 days in a row when the temperature rose above 49 °C.

It is much hotter on Venus. The Space probes measured surface temperatures on Venus of 462 °C.

Object or event	Temperature in °C
Kitchen fridge	4
Kitchen freezer	−20
Bunsen burner blue flame	1500
Melting point of nitrogen	−210
Boiling point of nitrogen	−196
Melting point of ethanol (alcohol)	−117
Boiling point of ethanol (alcohol)	79
Melting point of mercury	−39
Boiling point of mercury	357
Human body	37

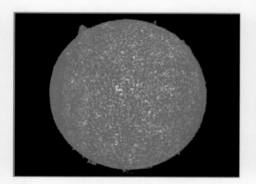

The surface of the Sun is at 5000 °C.

Lightning is at 30 000 °C.

e Would nitrogen be a solid, a liquid or a gas:

i on Triton? **ii** on Venus?

Questions

1. **a** Make a list of all the temperatures on these two pages. There are 19.
   b Put them in order with the coldest at the bottom and the hottest at the top.
   c Ignore the top three, and put all the others on one temperature scale. Use graph paper and use 2 cm for every 100 °C.
   d Write in the object or event next to its temperature.

2. Glass thermometers contain a liquid. If the liquid inside them freezes or boils, they will not work. Some glass thermometers contain mercury and others contain ethanol (alcohol). Information about mercury and ethanol is given in the table. Explain which type of thermometer you would choose to use:
   a on a summer day in Death Valley
   b on a winter day in Antarctica.

3. Draw diagrams to show the arrangement of the particles in nitrogen:
   a at −250 °C **b** at −200 °C **c** at −50 °C.

What temperature?

Internal energy

All matter is made up of particles. When you heat something, the particles move more – they have more kinetic energy. When you cool the object, the particles move less – they have less kinetic energy. This is shown in the diagram. The particles are vibrating more in the hotter solid.

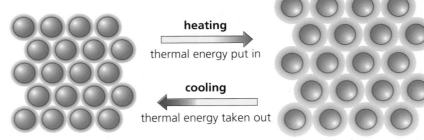

heating
thermal energy put in

cooling
thermal energy taken out

At lower temperatures the particles have less kinetic energy.

At higher temperatures the particles have more kinetic energy.

a Give two differences between the cooler solid and the hotter solid.

b Give two similarities between the cooler solid and the hotter solid.

Each particle in the hotter solid has more kinetic energy. When we add together the kinetic energy of all the particles, there is more energy in the hotter solid than in the cooler solid. The energy in the material because of the kinetic energy of the particles is called the **internal energy**. In the diagram, the hotter solid has more internal energy than the cooler solid.

Same temperature, different energy

Objects can be at the same temperature but contain very different amounts of internal energy. It depends on the number of particles. This is shown in the experiment described below.

You have two different sized cubes of iron. One cube has a volume of 1 cm³ and the other has a volume of 8 cm³. The two cubes are at the same temperature, both at 1000 °C. You drop each cube into a large container of water.

The results are shown in the diagram. The smaller cube heats the water to 28 °C. The bigger cube heats the water to 84 °C. The bigger cube heats the water more.

The bigger cube gave more energy to the water than the smaller cube. This means that, at 1000 °C, the bigger cube had more energy than the smaller cube. This is because there are more particles in the bigger cube. Each of these particles is vibrating, so each particle has some energy to give to the water particles. The more particles of iron there are, the more energy there is to give to the water.

c What would you have used to heat the cubes of iron?

d Which would have taken longer to heat to 1000 °C, the 1 cm³ cube or the 8 cm³ cube?

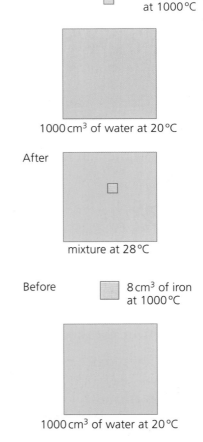

Before — 1 cm³ of iron at 1000 °C

1000 cm³ of water at 20 °C

After

mixture at 28 °C

Before — 8 cm³ of iron at 1000 °C

1000 cm³ of water at 20 °C

After

mixture at 84 °C

What is temperature?

The two cubes of iron were at the same temperature, but they had different amounts of energy to give to the water. This is because the internal energy (the total amount of energy inside the iron) is not the same as the temperature.

You can think about it like children with money. Each child has 5p. If there are 100 children in the playground, then there is 500p or £5 in the playground. If there are 10 children in the playground, then there is 50p. The total money in the playground represents the energy in the material. The money per child represents the temperature.

Think about the experiment again. Both cubes of iron were at the same temperature. They both contained the same amount of energy per particle. However, the bigger cube had more particles, so it contained more energy.

e Which would have more energy out of these pairs?

   i 1 g of molten lead at 400 °C or 1 kg of molten lead at 400 °C

   ii 1 g of ice at –20 °C or 1 kg of ice at –20 °C

Questions

1. Write out each scientific word along with its correct definition.

Word	Definition
temperature	one-hundredth of the temperature change between the freezing point and boiling point of water
cold	
boiling point	the temperature at which a substance changes from a liquid to a gas
internal energy	
degree Celsius	when the kinetic energy of the particles in a substance is low
	the total kinetic energy of the particles in a substance
	the amount of kinetic energy per particle in a substance

2. Look back at the experiment described on the opposite page, about the iron cubes being dropped into the water.

  a What happened to the particles of iron when the cubes were dropped into the water?

  b What happened to the particles of water when the iron cube was dropped in?

  c Explain, in your own words, why the second mixture ended up at 84 °C, while the first mixture only ended up at 28 °C.

When you revise

The **internal energy** of an object is the total kinetic energy of its particles.

When you heat something up, you give more kinetic energy to its particles.

The **temperature** of an object depends on the kinetic energy per particle.

Two objects at the same temperature but with different numbers of particles will contain different amounts of internal energy.

6.3 Transferring thermal energy

Hot things cool

You can poke a fire with a poker. One end of the poker is in the fire and the other is in your hand, but you are quite safe. However, if you leave the poker in the fire, the handle heats up. Thermal energy is transferred along the poker from the hot end to the cooler end.

If you take a pie out of the oven, it cools. The pie becomes cooler, and the air around the pie becomes hotter. If the pie is left in the oven, and the oven is left on, the pie stays hot. The pie cools because there is a temperature difference between the pie and the surrounding air. Thermal energy is transferred from the pie to the air, from the hotter object to the cooler object.

The Sun is very hot, with a surface temperature of over 5000 °C. The Earth is much cooler. Thermal energy is transferred from the hotter Sun to the cooler Earth.

a Explain why a cup of tea cools faster in a cold room than in a warm room.

The three examples above all show thermal energy being transferred from a hotter material to a cooler material. When the poker heated up in the fire, the thermal energy was transferred through a solid. This is an example of **conduction**.

Conduction

Conduction happens when thermal energy is transferred from particle to particle. Think about the poker again. The end that is in the fire is hotter than the rest. On the left, where the temperature is higher, the particles have more energy and vibrate more. On the right, where the temperature is lower, the particles have less energy and vibrate less.

1. The particles that vibrate more, at the hot end, hit against the neighbouring particles.

2. The particles that are hit vibrate more, so the temperature of that part of the poker rises.

3. The energy is passed from particle to particle, until all the particles are vibrating the same amount.

4. Conduction stops when the temperature is equal throughout the poker.

during conduction
transfer of energy

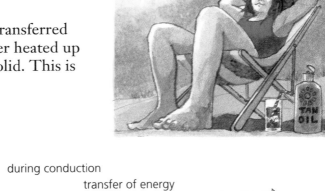

hotter end · colder end

after conduction
equal temperature throughout solid

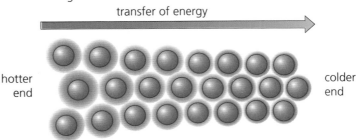

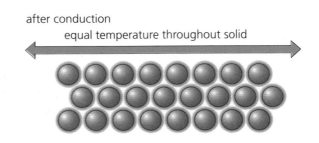

Conduction works best in solids, where the particles are touching and each particle touches many neighbours. In liquids, the particles are touching, but each particle has fewer neighbours to hit against. Conduction is very poor in gases. This is because the particles are far apart in a gas.

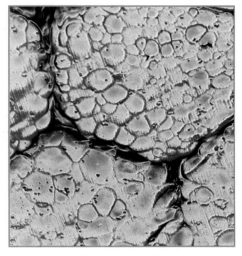

b Look at the diagrams opposite showing the particles in a solid, a liquid and a gas. Pick out a particle in:

i the solid   **ii** the liquid   **iii** the gas.

How many other particles are touching your chosen particle?

c Why do solids conduct thermal energy better than gases?

Thermal conductors and thermal insulators

All solids transfer energy by conduction, but some are better conductors than others. Metals are good thermal conductors and non-metals are poor thermal conductors. We say that non-metals are thermal insulators. The one common exception is graphite, a form of carbon (a non-metal) that is a good thermal conductor.

Non-metal materials that contain gas pockets are particularly good thermal insulators. These include expanded polystyrene, woolly jumpers, cavity wall insulation, the gas layer in double glazing and fluffed up feathers.

d **i** List five good thermal conductors.

ii List five poor thermal conductors.

e Why are gases particularly poor thermal conductors?

Expanded polystyrene contains pockets of air.

Questions

1. Mark comes home from school and finds these instructions from his dad on how to defrost a frozen chicken.

   ♦ Take off the plastic wrapper.

   ♦ Take it off the expanded polystyrene tray.

   ♦ Put the chicken on the drainer of the stainless steel sink, with the skin in contact with the metal.

   Use your knowledge of conduction to explain why Mark's dad left these instructions.

2. Explain why kebabs cook more quickly on metal skewers than:

   a with no skewers   **b** on wooden skewers.

3. There are two pokers. They are the same length and made of the same metal. One is much wider and heavier than the other. The pointed end of each is put in the fire. Which handle would become too hot to hold first? Give reasons for your answer.

When you revise

Thermal energy is transferred from hotter objects to cooler objects.

Conduction is one of the ways in which thermal energy is transferred.

In conduction, energy is transferred from one particle to the particles touching it, from hotter to colder.

77

Transferring more thermal energy

Moving air

Look at the picture of a hot pie cooling. The pie is surrounded by air. The thermal energy is carried away from the pie by the air.

The particles in the air carry away the thermal energy. The air particles near the pie heat up and move more – they get more kinetic energy. These particles then move away and other particles take their place. This happens again and again, until the pie is the same temperature as the air. Transferring thermal energy by moving particles is called **convection**. It happens in gases and liquids, because the particles in gases and liquids can move about.

a Why doesn't convection happen in solids?

Look at the photo. If the man puts his hand above **B**, it feels hot. This is because hot air is rising up the chimney from **A** to **B**. The smoke falls from **C** to **D**. This is because colder air is dropping down from **C** to **D**, carrying the smoke. Thermal energy is being transferred away from the candle flame by convection.

b Look at the photo. What will happen to the smoke when it reaches **A**?

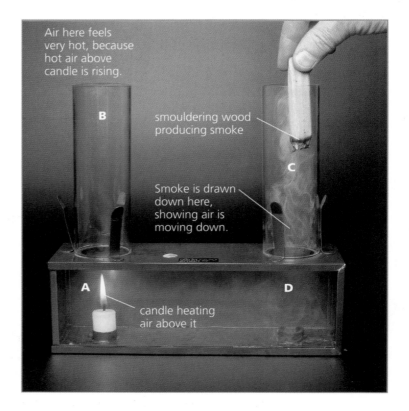

Air here feels very hot, because hot air above candle is rising.

B

smouldering wood producing smoke

Smoke is drawn down here, showing air is moving down.

C

A

D

candle heating air above it

Convection currents

Convection always happens in two parts. The hotter gas or liquid rises, and the colder gas or liquid falls. Look back at the experiment.

1. The hotter air at **A** rises.
2. The air at **B** is pushed out of the chimney.
3. The cooler air at **C** falls.
4. The air at **D** is pushed around to replace the air at **A**.

This movement of air is a **convection current**. Convection currents can happen in gases and liquids.

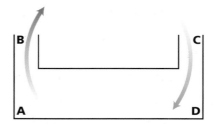

Look back at the convection current on the opposite page.

c Why does the air at **A** rise?

d Why does the air at **C** fall?

e What do we call the circle of rising and falling air?

f What will happen to the temperature of the air in the box?

Convection in liquids

Convection also happens in liquids. Look at the left-hand photo of the beaker. The beaker contains water, which is being heated at one side. The water above the Bunsen burner is hotter, so it rises. The rising water is shown by the purple dye.

The photo on the right shows the beaker a short time later. Purple dye has moved across the top and will soon start to fall on the right-hand side. This is because the water away from the Bunsen burner is cooler. This cold water falls, carrying the purple dye. The dye shows the convection current in the liquid.

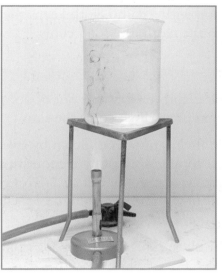

Convection happens because one part of the liquid or gas is hotter than another. Once the temperature evens out, the convection current stops.

g What would happen if the Bunsen burner were taken away before the temperature evened out?

Questions

1. Imagine a room with a heater in one corner. Explain how the heater heats the air in the whole room. Use a diagram in your explanation and these words:

   convection   convection current   rise   fall

2. Look at the photo of the smoke box.

   a Use your knowledge about particles to draw the following diagrams:

   i the air particles at **A**   **ii** the air particles at **C**.

   Use the same size box to contain the particles you draw.

   b What is between the particles in your diagrams?

   c Which would have the greater mass, the air at **A** or the air at **C**?

When you revise

In **convection** the particles move, transferring the thermal energy.

Convection happens in gases and liquids, but not in solids.

A **convection current** happens when one part of a gas or liquid is hotter than another part.

Transferring even more thermal energy

Suddenly cooler

You feel cold if you stand around while you are wet. You may have felt this after swimming, or after a bath. Drying off the water with a towel stops this happening. Covering food with a damp cloth keeps the food cool. As the water evaporates from the cloth, the food cools.

Keeping cool

We sweat to cool down. Our sweat glands push water out of our pores, onto the skin. The water then evaporates which cools the skin.

Dogs do not have sweat glands, so they cannot cool down by sweating. Instead they pant. They hang their tongues out of their mouths, and breathe in and out quickly, pushing air across the wet surface of their tongues. Blood is flowing through the tongue. The blood cools down and the cooler blood then flows around the body.

a What will happen to the water on the surface of the dog's tongue?

b Why does pushing air over the tongue help cool the dog?

Radiation

Thermal energy is transferred from the Sun to the Earth. This cannot happen by conduction or convection, because there are no particles in the empty space between the Earth and the Sun. The thermal energy is transferred by a process called **radiation**. Radiation is the transfer of thermal energy without particles. During radiation, **infrared radiation** carries thermal energy from a hotter object to a cooler object.

Infrared radiation is like light in many ways:

♦ The infrared radiation is given out by a source, like light is given out by a source.
♦ It spreads out in all directions.
♦ Any hot object is a source of infrared radiation.

Look at the photo of people next to a car. The picture was not taken using light, because the scene was too dark. It was taken with an infrared camera, which picks up infrared radiation rather than light. The people show up brightly, because they are sources of infrared radiation.

The Sun produces infrared radiation that heats the Earth. The radiation can travel across the emptiness of space because, like light, it does not need a material to travel through.

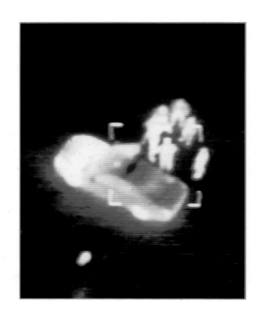

Infrared radiation is like light in other ways. Like light, it is reflected by some surfaces and absorbed by others. Matt black surfaces absorb infrared radiation best, while shiny silver surfaces reflect it best.

Look at the photo of the athlete wrapped in the shiny survival blanket. The athlete is giving off thermal energy by radiation. One way in which the blanket keeps her warm is by reflecting back the infrared radiation onto her skin.

c The Earth is not heated by conduction or convection.

   i Why not?

   ii What type of thermal energy transfer heats the Earth?

All methods at once

Look at the diagram opposite of a cup of tea cooling. The four different coloured arrows show the four methods by which thermal energy is being transferred away from the hot cup of tea. These are conduction, convection, evaporation and radiation.

d **i** Which arrows show thermal energy transfer through a solid?

   ii What method of thermal energy transfer is this?

e **i** Which arrows only come from the surface of the liquid?

   ii What method of thermal energy transfer is this?

f **i** Which arrows show thermal energy transfer using convection?

   ii Why are these arrows curly?

g **i** Which arrows show the transfer of thermal energy from the mug of tea in all directions?

   ii What method of thermal energy transfer is this?

Questions

1. Explain why a person wearing a black T-shirt on a sunny day is hotter than a person wearing a white T-shirt.

2. Taz and Mary are studying the food containers used by take-away restaurants. The Chinese restaurant uses aluminium foil containers with cardboard lids. The fish and chip shop wraps the food in three layers of paper.

   a How does each type of packaging prevent loss of thermal energy by:

      i conduction?   **ii** convection?   **iii** radiation?

   b Design your own packaging to keep take-away food hot.

When you revise

Thermal energy can be lost from a liquid by evaporation. The liquid then cools its surroundings.

Radiation happens when thermal energy is transferred by **infrared radiation**, which is like light.

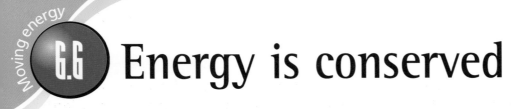

6.6 Energy is conserved

Learn about

- Energy transfers
- Energy conservation
- Energy dissipation

Energy transfers

When anything is happening, energy is transferred. Energy can be transferred as light energy, sound energy, electrical energy, kinetic energy and thermal energy. Energy is measured in joules, J. We often measure energy in kilojoules, kJ, or megajoules, MJ.

Energy can be stored as chemical energy, strain energy and gravitational energy. Stretched or squashed materials store strain energy. Food, fuels and batteries store chemical energy. Objects that have been lifted up store gravitational energy. Another term for gravitational energy is **gravitational potential energy** or **potential energy**.

Energy transfer diagrams show *where* and *how* energy is transferred.

a Draw an energy transfer diagram for:
  i a battery-powered radio
  ii a catapult.

b How many joules are there in: **i** 1 kJ? **ii** 1 MJ?

Energy conservation

Energy is moved from place to place, but it is very rarely created or destroyed. This means that the energy going into something should be the same as the energy coming out of it. So we say that energy is conserved.

Look at the circuit with the two batteries and a lamp. The energy entering and leaving the circuit can be shown using an energy transfer diagram.

c What type of energy is stored in the battery?

d How does the electrical energy get to the lamp?

e What happens at the lamp?

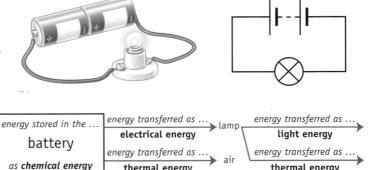

The energy transfer diagram shows *where* and *how* the energy is transferred, but it does not show *how much* energy is being transferred. This means it does not show that the energy is conserved.

We can use a different type of diagram to show energy conservation. The diagram to the right shows the energy transfers in the same circuit. In this diagram, the width of each arrow shows the amount of energy.

This diagram shows very clearly that the energy is conserved. 100 J enters the circuit from the battery. The energy leaving the circuit can be added up, as shown opposite:

So the energy entering equals the energy leaving. The energy is conserved.

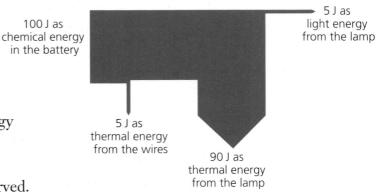

```
    5 J   as thermal energy from the wires
+ 90 J   as thermal energy from the lamp
 + 5 J   as light energy from the lamp
─────────
 100 J   total energy leaving circuit
```

'Wasted' energy

Not all the energy ends up where we want it. Look at the energy transfer diagrams for the circuit. Only a small amount of the energy ends up as light energy. The rest ends up as thermal energy. We did not want this thermal energy, we wanted the light energy. The 'wasted' energy heats up the air around the circuit. We say that this energy is **dissipated**. Dissipated means spread about.

f Look at the energy transfer diagram that shows the amount of energy being transferred.

   i How much energy ended up as light energy?

   ii How much energy was put into the circuit?

   iii Where did the rest of the energy end up?

   iv How much of the energy was dissipated (spread about in the air)?

Questions

1. Pair up the beginnings and ends of the sentences. Write out the sentences.

Beginnings	Ends
The amount of energy going in …	… we say it is dissipated.
Dissipated energy is usually spread about in the air …	… energy is transferred, but rarely created and never destroyed.
	… makes things work.
Energy conservation happens because …	… as thermal energy.
When energy gets spread about …	… equals the amount of energy coming out.
Energy …	

2. Study the diagram showing how much energy enters and leaves a hairdryer.

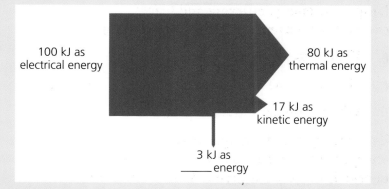

   a Where does the hairdryer get the energy needed to make it work?

   b How much energy enters the hairdryer?

   c How much energy leaves the hairdryer as thermal energy?

   d How much energy leaves the hairdryer as kinetic energy?

   e How much energy leaves the hairdryer in another way?

   f How much energy leaves the hairdryer altogether?

   g What do you notice about your answer to questions **b** and **f**?

   h Think about using a hairdryer. What type of energy is the 3 kJ at the bottom of the diagram?

When you revise

Energy is transferred from place to place, but conserved.

Not all the energy is transferred to where we want it. A lot of it ends up as thermal energy.

Once the thermal energy is **dissipated**, it becomes less useful.

6.7 Heating and floating

Moving energy

Think about

♦ Changing more than one variable

Raising the temperature

Ellen and Sean heated different sized blocks of three different metals. They wanted to find out how much energy it takes to raise the temperature by 40 °C, from 25 °C to 65 °C.

Sean plotted a scatter graph of their results. His graph is shown below. Ellen and Sean discussed what lines to put on their graph. Sean did not think there was a pattern, and he did not want to draw lines on the graph. Ellen thought there should be three lines – one for copper, one for aluminium and one for tin.

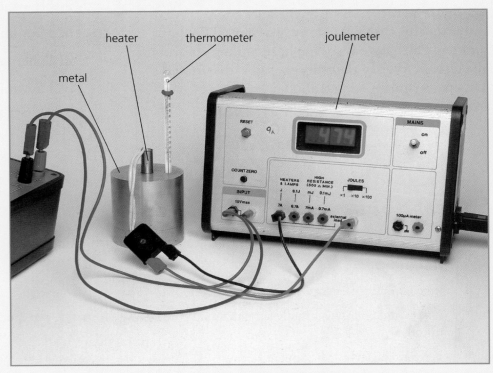

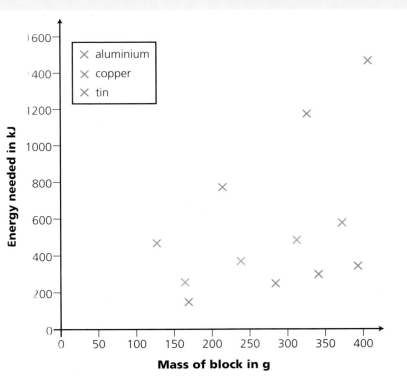

a Who do you agree with, Sean or Ellen? Give reasons for your answer.

b How does increasing the mass change the energy needed to heat the block?

c How does changing the metal change the energy needed to heat the block?

d Use the graph (without drawing on the book!) to estimate how much energy would be needed to heat 200 g of aluminium by 40 °C.

The energy needed to heat the block by 40 °C depends on the type of metal *and* the mass of the metal. 300 kJ of energy will heat 83 g of aluminium, or 194 g of copper, or 346 g of tin, by 40 °C.

Rising and sinking

Justin and Yasmin were taking part in a Science Challenge. The challenge was to make a balloon that would float where it was put, neither rising nor sinking.

Each team was given eight balloons that had been set up by the organisers. Each balloon was labelled with the volume of gas inside and the total mass of the balloon. Some of the balloons sank and some of them rose up towards the ceiling.

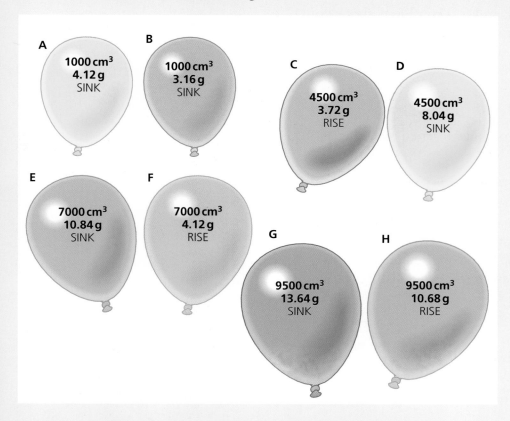

e Justin said, 'Heavy balloons sink and light balloons rise.' Find three pairs of balloons in the diagram that support Justin's idea. Why did you choose them?

f Yasmin said, 'Big balloons rise and small balloons sink.' Find one pair of balloons in the diagram that supports Yasmin's idea. Why did you choose them?

g Suggest what Yasmin and Justin can do to make one of the balloons in the diagram float for the Science Challenge. (There is more than one solution to the problem.)

h What two variables can affect whether a balloon sinks or rises?

Questions

1. Look at the diagram opposite. It shows three of the winning balloons from the challenge. All the winning balloons floated in the room without rising or sinking.

  a Which balloon has the greatest mass?

  b Which balloon has the greatest volume?

  c Which balloon has the smallest mass?

  d Which balloon has the smallest volume?

  e Do this calculation for each balloon:

$$\frac{\text{mass}}{\text{volume}}$$

  f What do you notice about the answers to the calculations?

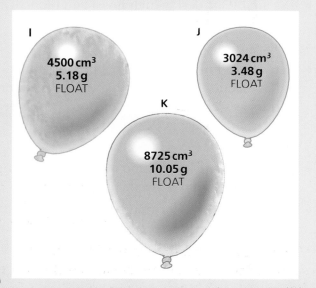

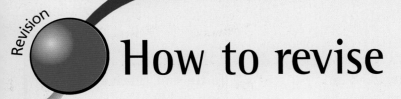

How to revise

Key Stage 3 tests

At the end of Year 9 you will do a Key Stage 3 test which covers everything you have studied over the last three years. It is an opportunity for you to show how much you have learned over the course. To help you get a good mark and feel confident about doing the test, it is a good idea to revise thoroughly before the test. Your teacher will probably help you with this in science lessons, but there is a lot you can do yourself using the revision section of this book.

What to revise

You need to revise everything that you have learned over the last three years. This book will help you.

♦ It contains three revision units covering biology, chemistry and physics topics from Years 7 and 8 which you need to revise.

♦ It also contains six units of new Year 9 material which you need to revise. Look back at the 'When you revise' boxes at the ends of the spreads in the first six units – these give you the key points to remember. The blue revision boxes on the pages also revise some material from Years 7 and 8.

Where to revise

♦ It is best to revise in a room with no distractions like a TV, music or people busy doing other things.

♦ Most people find it best to have a quiet place for revising.

♦ Use a table or desk which gives you plenty of space to lay out your books and notes.

♦ Make sure you have a good source of light to read by.

♦ Get yourself organised – have plenty of blank paper and a selection of pens and pencils in different colours as well as the notes or books you need.

When to revise

♦ Try to set aside some time early each evening. Don't leave it too late so that your brain is tired.

♦ Revise for about 15 minutes and then take a 5-minute break. You could perhaps allow yourself to listen to a song (only one!). Then do another 15 minutes' revision and have another short break. Revise for another 15 minutes, and then have a longer break.

♦ Breaking up your revision into small chunks like this is much better than revising for a solid hour without any breaks. You will remember more this way.

♦ Keep a clock close by to help you keep track of the time.

Revision timetables

- Don't try to revise your entire science course in one night!
- Plan your revision long before your test.
- Work out how you will divide the material up, and how much you will revise each night.
- Work out how many evenings you will have available for revision.
- Make a timetable something like this to make sure you cover every topic at least once.

Day	What I will revise	Tick when done
Day 1	Topic 1	
Day 2	Topic 2	
Day 3	Topic 3	

How to revise

There are many different techniques that you can use. Here are just a few.

1 Read – Cover – Write – Check

   Read an entire double page spread in the book. Then close the book and write notes on as many key points as you can remember. Then open the book again, check what you wrote down and go over the things you didn't remember. Repeat this until you can remember everything on the pages.

2 Make a memory map for each section. Then try to learn the memory map – think about the way each part of it is linked together. Then cover the map up and try to redraw it. The last question on each revision spread suggests you do this.

3 Write out lots of questions. Then close the book and see if you can answer them. You can also get someone else to ask you the questions. There are some questions on the revision pages to get you going. At the end of each revision unit are example test questions with tips from the examiners about the best way to answer.

4 Make sure you know the meanings of all the key words you come across. The first question on each revision spread suggests you do this.

5 Make up silly rhymes or mnemonics for important facts or patterns. The sillier they are, the easier it will be for your brain to remember them.

Don't just sit there with a book in front of you. It's not the best way to learn. The best way to revise is by actively doing tasks to make your brain work. This will make it much easier to remember things. Then you can go into your test confident that you will do the best you can.

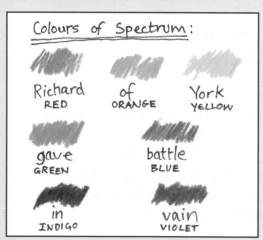

Colours of Spectrum:

Richard — RED
of — ORANGE
York — YELLOW
gave — GREEN
battle — BLUE
in — INDIGO
vain — VIOLET

7.1 Cells and organs

Cells

All living things are made up of small building blocks called **cells**. There are two main types of cell: **animal cells** and **plant cells**. These have a lot in common, but there are also some differences.

> **Remember:** you must be able to label diagrams of cells.

Animal cells

Animal cells have three main structures: the **cell membrane**, the **nucleus** and the **cytoplasm**.

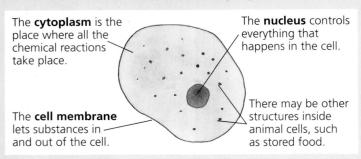

The **cytoplasm** is the place where all the chemical reactions take place.

The **nucleus** controls everything that happens in the cell.

The **cell membrane** lets substances in and out of the cell.

There may be other structures inside animal cells, such as stored food.

Plant cells

A plant cell also has a cell membrane, a nucleus and cytoplasm. Unlike animal cells, it also has a **cell wall**, **chloroplasts** and a large **vacuole**.

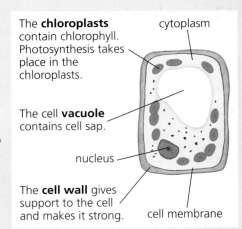

The **chloroplasts** contain chlorophyll. Photosynthesis takes place in the chloroplasts.

cytoplasm

The cell **vacuole** contains cell sap.

nucleus

The **cell wall** gives support to the cell and makes it strong.

cell membrane

a Make a table showing the differences between an animal cell and a plant cell.

Cells adapted to their functions

Cells are adapted to their functions in different ways. You need to know about the following examples: sperm cells, egg cells, root hair cells and epithelial cells.

b Make a table of the different types of cell shown opposite. Include one column for adaptations and one column for functions.

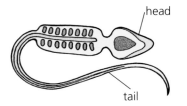

head

tail

Sperm cells have long **tails** to swim to the egg and a **pointed head** which helps them burrow into the egg.

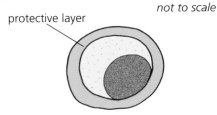

not to scale

protective layer

Egg cells have a protective layer so that just one sperm can get through.

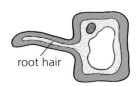

root hair

Root hair cells have a long finger-like root hair which gives a very large surface area to absorb water.

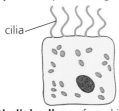

cilia

Epithelial cells are found in your nose and throat. They produce mucus to trap dust and germs.

Tissues

When a group of similar cells carries out a particular function we call the group of cells a **tissue**.

- Examples of tissues in animals, such as humans, include muscle tissue and nerve tissue.
- Examples of tissues in plants include onion skin tissue and palisade tissue.

Organs

When a group of two or more tissues work together they form an **organ**.

- Examples of organs in animals, such as humans, include the heart, lungs, stomach, eyes and brain.
- Examples of organs in plants include leaves, stems, roots and petals.

Organ systems

When a group of organs work together they form an **organ system**. Examples include:

♦ in animals, such as humans – the circulatory system, the reproductive system, the skeletal system and the digestive system.

♦ in plants – a flower.

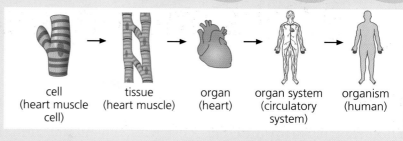

cell (heart muscle cell) → tissue (heart muscle) → organ (heart) → organ system (circulatory system) → organism (human)

c Make a table showing one example of a cell, a tissue, an organ and an organ system for plants and one for animals.

The skeletal system

The **skeletal system** or skeleton is an organ system. The skeleton is made up of over 200 **bones** and is important because it:

♦ allows the animal to move
♦ protects important organs like the brain
♦ provides the animal with support.

Bones come together at **joints**, which allow the bones to move.

♦ The bones are held together at a joint by **ligaments**.
♦ There are three types of joint: **hinge**, **ball and socket** and **pivot**.
♦ Friction is reduced at the joints as they contain **cartilage**.
♦ Bones need **muscles** to move them.

d Make a table showing the various parts of the skeletal system and their functions: bones, muscles, ligaments and cartilage.

Muscles are joined onto bones by special fibres called **tendons**.

♦ Muscles are made of muscle tissue, which can **contract** and **relax**.
♦ Bones move when a muscle contracts.
♦ Muscles can only pull, they cannot push, so they work in **antagonistic pairs**.

e Explain how an antagonistic pair of muscles works.

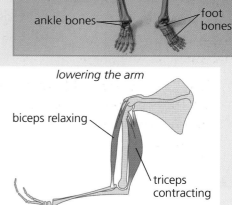

skull
collar bone
jaw bone
shoulder joint
shoulder blade
breast bone
ribs
humerus
vertebrae
radius
wrist bones
ulna
hip joint
hand bones
pelvis
femur (thigh)
knee joint
knee cap
tibia (shin)
fibula
foot bones
ankle bones

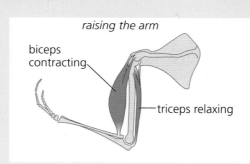

raising the arm
biceps contracting
triceps relaxing

lowering the arm
biceps relaxing
triceps contracting

Questions

1. Make a list of all the key words on this spread with their meanings.

2. For each of the following, decide whether it is a part of a cell, a type of cell, a tissue, an organ or an organ system:

   a heart **b** skeleton **c** chloroplast **d** sperm
   e leaf   **f** petal   **g** ear.

3. Explain why a flower is an organ system.

4. What are the functions of the human skeleton?

5. Describe the cells, tissues and organs that make up the circulatory system.

6. Draw a memory map to help you remember the information about cells, tissues, organs and organ systems.

Nutrition

Food

Food contains many different substances. The useful substances that food contains are called **nutrients**. Plants and animals get their food in different ways. Plants make their own food by a process called **photosynthesis**. Animals are **consumers** and eat plants, other animals or both plants and animals. Animals and plants get energy from their food by the process called **respiration**.

Balanced diets

Your body needs nutrients to give it energy and to keep it working properly. A diet that gives the body the right amounts of all the nutrients is called a **balanced diet**. This consists of:

- **carbohydrates**, for example in bread, for energy
- **fats**, such as those in milk and butter, for energy and insulation
- **proteins**, for example in meat, fish and nuts, for growth and repair
- **vitamins** and **minerals** to keep different parts of the body healthy
- **water**, in which all the chemical reactions in your body take place
- **fibre** to keep the food moving through the gut.

Vitamins and minerals

When the body doesn't get the required amount of a nutrient, such as a vitamin or a mineral, it is **deficient** in that nutrient. This can cause ill health, for example:

- vitamin C, found in fruits such as blackcurrants and green vegetables such as cabbage, stops people getting scurvy
- the mineral calcium, found in food such as milk, is needed for strong bones and teeth to develop.

Digestion

- When you eat food, the large molecules need to be broken down into very small molecules. This is called **digestion** and it takes place in the **digestive system**.
- Only small molecules can dissolve and pass through the lining of the small intestine into the blood.
- Large molecules that are insoluble cannot pass through the lining, and need to be broken down further.

a Make a table to show all the nutrients that make up a balanced diet. Include a column to show which foods each one comes from. Include another column to say why the nutrient is needed.

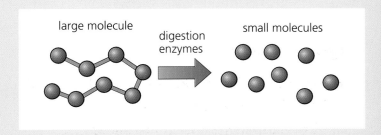

large molecule   digestion enzymes   small molecules

b Write a paragraph explaining why large food molecules have to be broken down in the body.

Where does digestion happen?

♦ Digestion starts in the **mouth**, and carries on all the way through the **stomach** and **small intestine**.

♦ Food spends several hours in the stomach, where acidic digestive juices help break the food down.

♦ The food is pushed through the gut by a process called **peristalsis**.

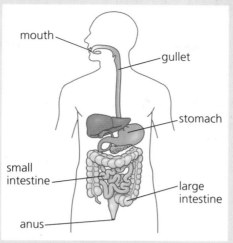

♦ In the small intestine, pancreatic and intestinal juices digest several different types of nutrients. Alkaline **bile** neutralises the acid from the stomach and helps to break down fats.

♦ Any waste food that is left is removed from the body through the **anus**.

Breaking food down

♦ In the mouth, the teeth help break up the food into smaller pieces. This mechanical breakdown of the food is a **physical process**.

♦ In digestion, substances called **enzymes** help to break the larger molecules into smaller molecules. Breaking down food in this way is a **chemical process**.

Absorption

♦ The small intestine has a very large surface area as it is made up of millions of tiny finger-like structures called **villi** (one villus).

♦ The large surface ensures that the digested food passes from the intestine into the blood quickly. This process is called **absorption**.

♦ The undigested food, that is mainly fibre, passes into the large intestine because its molecules are too large to be absorbed.

♦ Water is absorbed in the **large intestine** and waste food can be stored here before it is pushed out from the body through the anus. This process is called **egestion**.

d Draw a flow diagram to show how food is digested and absorbed by the body. Start at the mouth and finish where undigested food leaves the body. Add labels to explain briefly what happens to the food at each stage.

c Write a short paragraph to describe how food is broken down. Use the following words: physical, chemical, mouth, enzymes, teeth, stomach.

Questions

1. Make a list of all the key words on this spread with their meanings.

2. What nutrients make up a balanced diet?

3. What is protein used for in the body?

4. Explain the following statements.
   a Enzymes are very important in digestion.
   b Fibre passes out of the body undigested.

5. Draw a memory map to help you remember the information about food and digestion.

Photosynthesis and respiration

Photosynthesis

♦ **Photosynthesis** happens in the green parts of a plant, usually the leaves.

♦ The green parts contain **chloroplasts** which are green because they contain the chemical **chlorophyll**.

Photosynthesis can be summarised by the word equation:

carbon dioxide + water → glucose + oxygen **energy is taken in**

♦ Plants take in carbon dioxide through holes in the leaves called **stomata**.

♦ Water is taken in from the soil through the **root hairs**.

♦ Light energy from the Sun is absorbed by chlorophyll.

♦ Glucose and oxygen are produced. Oxygen leaves through the stomata. The glucose is used to provide energy for the plant.

♦ Photosynthesis produces the **biomass** of the plant. Biomass increases with growth. Biomass is the total mass of a living thing not including the water.

Transport in plants

♦ Glucose is transported from the leaves to the rest of the plant in the veins.

♦ Water for photosynthesis is transported from the roots to the leaves in the veins.

Plant nutrients

Minerals are also taken in by the root hairs. The most important plant minerals are:

♦ **nitrogen**, as nitrate salts, needed to make proteins for growth

♦ **phosphorus**, as phosphate salts, needed to make the roots grow properly

♦ **potassium**, needed to make chlorophyll. Without potassium the leaves would turn yellow so photosynthesis could not happen.

Respiration in plants

Plants break down the glucose they produce to release the chemical energy stored in it. Glucose reacts with oxygen to produce carbon dioxide and water. Energy is given out in the reaction. This is called **respiration** and can be summarised by the word equation:

glucose + oxygen → carbon dioxide + water **energy is given out**

Remember: you must learn this word equation.

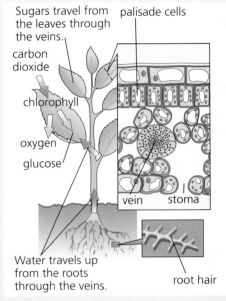

Sugars travel from the leaves through the veins.

palisade cells

carbon dioxide

chlorophyll

oxygen

glucose

vein   stoma

Water travels up from the roots through the veins.

root hair

a Where does the plant get carbon dioxide and water from? What happens to the oxygen and glucose made in photosynthesis?

b Make a table listing the main plant nutrients and why they are important.

Remember: the plant nutrients Never Push Pandas.

Remember: you must learn this word equation.

- Glucose comes from photosynthesis. Oxygen comes from photosynthesis during the day and from the air at night.
- Carbon dioxide and water are released through the stomata.

Respiration in humans

Food gives you energy. Carbohydrates, fats and proteins provide the body with the sources of energy you need to stay healthy. Energy is released from food by respiration. The word equation is the same as for plants. Respiration takes place inside all living cells of plants, animals and bacteria.

c Describe respiration using the following words: energy, glucose, muscles, cells.

- The fuel used in respiration is glucose. It is obtained from the digestion of food.
- The oxygen for respiration comes from breathing in.
- Carbon dioxide and water are produced and are released when you breathe out.
- The energy is used for many things, such as working your muscles.

Transport in the blood

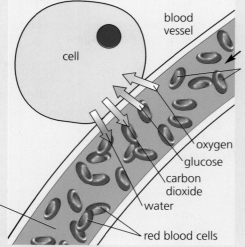

Carbon dioxide and water are made during respiration. They are taken away from the respiring cells in the blood. Carbon dioxide is dissolved in the blood.

blood vessel

cell

The oxygen and glucose for respiration are transported to the cells by the blood.

Oxygen is attached to the **haemoglobin** in red blood cells and glucose is dissolved in the blood.

oxygen
glucose
carbon dioxide
water
red blood cells

The blood carries carbon dioxide and water to the lungs where they are released.

Oxygen and glucose can pass out from the blood through the thin-walled capillaries to nearby cells where they are needed.

d In human respiration, where do the oxygen and glucose come from? How do humans get rid of the carbon dioxide and water produced?

Questions

1. Make a list of all the key words on this spread with their meanings.

2. Why is chlorophyll important for photosynthesis and where is it found?

3. Explain why both photosynthesis and respiration take place during the day but only respiration happens at night.

4. What differences might you expect to find in air that you breathed in and air that you breathed out?

5. Which nutrient would you give your plants to make sure the roots are healthy?

6. How are water and glucose transported around a plant?

7. Explain the following statements.
   a Pond weed in a fish tank helps the fish stay alive.
   b Nitrogen fertilisers make plants grow quicker.

8. Draw a memory map to help you remember the information about photosynthesis and respiration.

 7.4 Reproduction

Human reproduction

Male reproductive system:

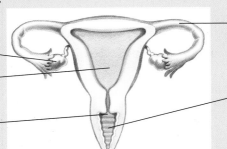

Sperm are made in the **testes**. There are two of these (one **testis**).

The testes are in a bag of skin called the **scrotum**.

The sperm leave the testes through a tube called the **sperm tube**.

Glands add a special liquid to the sperm to make **semen**.

Eventually the sperm travel down the **penis**. This is where they leave the man's body.

Female reproductive system:

The eggs or ova are made in the **ovaries**.

The **uterus** (womb) is where the baby will develop if the egg becomes fertilised.

The opening of the uterus is called the **cervix**.

Once a month an egg leaves one of the ovaries and travels down the **oviduct** to the **uterus**.

Sperm enter the woman's body through the **vagina**.

a Make a list of the parts of the male and female reproductive systems and their functions.

b Make a list of three changes that happen during puberty to: **i** boys **ii** girls.

Adolescence

Adolescence is a time in everyone's life when physical and emotional changes take place to prepare us to be young adults. **Puberty** is the first part of adolescence, when most of these changes take place.

Changes in boys	Changes in girls
Body hair, including pubic hair, starts to grow	Body hair, including pubic hair, starts to grow
Voice deepens	Breasts grow
Testes start to make sperm and hormones	Ovaries start to release eggs and make hormones
Shoulders broaden	Hips widen
Sexual organs get bigger	Periods start
Behaviour changes	Behaviour changes

Menstruation

At puberty, girls begin a monthly cycle called the **menstrual cycle**. Each cycle lasts about 28 days.

c Draw a flow diagram to show the main stages of the menstrual cycle. For each stage, write a label to describe what happens.

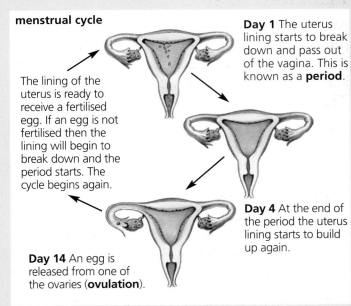

menstrual cycle

The lining of the uterus is ready to receive a fertilised egg. If an egg is not fertilised then the lining will begin to break down and the period starts. The cycle begins again.

Day 1 The uterus lining starts to break down and pass out of the vagina. This is known as a **period**.

Day 4 At the end of the period the uterus lining starts to build up again.

Day 14 An egg is released from one of the ovaries (**ovulation**).

Human fertilisation

- After **sexual intercourse**, the sperm start to swim from the vagina into the uterus. The sperm swim up into both oviducts. Many sperm will die on the way.

- If there is an egg in the oviduct: the sperm will surround it and the first sperm to reach the egg burrows into it. The nucleus of the sperm joins with the nucleus of the egg. This is called **fertilisation**. The fertilised egg will become a baby. The woman is pregnant. The menstrual cycle stops.

- If there is no egg in the oviduct: all the sperm will die in a short time. No baby will be produced. The menstrual cycle continues.

Pregnancy

- **Cell division**: about 24 hours after it has been fertilised, the egg divides into two cells, then into four cells. After four days it has divided into 32 cells. It is now called an **embryo**.

- **Implantation**: about a week after fertilisation, the embryo attaches to the wall of the uterus. This is called **implantation**.

The placenta

- The **placenta** provides the fetus with all the substances it needs from the mother.

- The **cord** joins the placenta to the fetus.

- The baby receives oxygen and food from the mother and gets rid of carbon dioxide and other waste through the placenta.

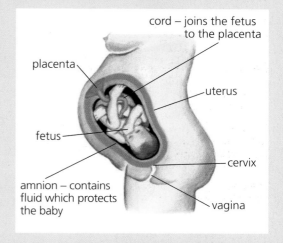

(d) Describe how the fertilised egg becomes an embryo.

Plant fertilisation

After pollination, a **pollen tube** grows to carry the **pollen grain** to the **egg cell**. Fertilisation takes place when the nucleus of the male sex cell, the pollen grain, joins with the nucleus of the female sex cell, the egg cell. This produces a fertilised egg cell.

(e) List the main stages in plant fertilisation.

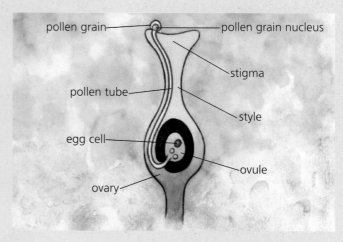

Questions

1. Make a list of all the key words on this spread with their meanings.

2. What is the function of the placenta?

3. What is the function of the amnion?

4. How are plant and human reproduction similar?

5. Draw a memory map to help you remember the information about reproduction in plants and animals.

Classification and variation

Classification

- All living things can be sorted into different groups depending on their features. The four main groups are **animals**, **plants**, **microorganisms** and **fungi**.
- The grouping of things is called **classification**.
- Animals are grouped into two main groups: **vertebrates**, animals with a backbone and **invertebrates**, animals without a backbone.

Vertebrates

Vertebrates are divided into five smaller groups:

a Make a table to show the main differences between the five groups of vertebrates.

- **Birds**, such as eagles and penguins, lay eggs with hard shells and look after their young when they are born. They have feathers and wings and most can fly.

- **Amphibians**, such as frogs and newts, lay jelly-like eggs in water. They breathe air and live part of their life in water and part on land.

- **Reptiles**, such as crocodiles and lizards, lay eggs with a leathery skin on land. They breathe air and live mainly on land.

- **Mammals**, such as humans and lions, develop inside the mother. The young are fed on milk from the mammary glands of the mother.

- **Fish**, such as sharks and cod, lay their eggs in water. They breathe through gills and live only in water.

Invertebrates

- There are seven main types of invertebrate: jellyfish, starfish, flatworms, roundworms, segmented worms, molluscs and **arthropods**.
- Arthropods are invertebrates with segmented bodies and lots of jointed legs.
- Arthropods themselves can be divided into four smaller groups, depending on their body type and the number of legs. The groups are crustaceans, centipedes and millipedes, spiders and insects.

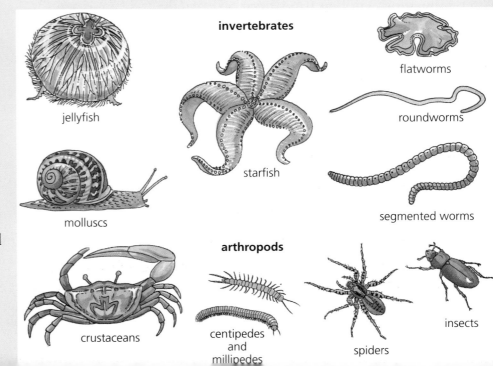

invertebrates

jellyfish

flatworms

roundworms

starfish

segmented worms

molluscs

arthropods

crustaceans

centipedes and millipedes

spiders

insects

Plants

There are many different types of plant on Earth. They are classified into four main groups that are found in different habitats:

b For each main plant group, write down one thing that would help you classify it.

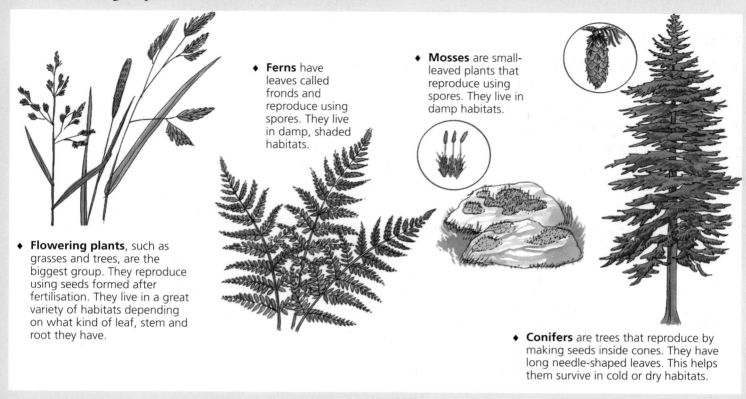

♦ **Ferns** have leaves called fronds and reproduce using spores. They live in damp, shaded habitats.

♦ **Mosses** are small-leaved plants that reproduce using spores. They live in damp habitats.

♦ **Flowering plants**, such as grasses and trees, are the biggest group. They reproduce using seeds formed after fertilisation. They live in a great variety of habitats depending on what kind of leaf, stem and root they have.

♦ **Conifers** are trees that reproduce by making seeds inside cones. They have long needle-shaped leaves. This helps them survive in cold or dry habitats.

Variation

♦ The differences between living things are called **variation**.

♦ When there are enough differences between groups of organisms we call them different **species**. All the different kinds of dog belong to the same species because they can mate and produce offspring. A dog and a cat are different species, as they cannot breed together.

Questions

1. Make a list of all the key words on this spread with their meanings.

2. What are the differences between:

   a a mammal and a bird?

   b an amphibian and a reptile?

3. How do you know that a mollusc is an invertebrate?

4. Make a key to identify different plants.

5. Why can't cats and dogs breed together?

6. Make a memory map to help you remember the information about classification and variation.

Thick layer of blubber insulates the body

thick white fur

Large feet spread the weight.

All the body fat is in the hump

Sandy colour provides camouflage.

Camels can store a lot of water in their bodies.

Large feet spread the weight on the sand.

The environment

Adaptation

- A **habitat** is the place where an organism lives.
- An **ecosystem** is an area like a pond or a forest including all the living things in it and its soil, air and climate.
- Different organisms are suited or **adapted** to their environment to help them survive in it.
- Polar bears have thick, white fur coats to insulate them from the cold. It is difficult to see the white polar bear against the snow because it is **camouflaged** against the snow so it cannot be seen by its prey.
- Camels are able to store water to help them survive in the hot desert. They have large feet to stop them sinking into the sand. They face the hot Sun at midday to expose the minimum body surface to the Sun's rays.

a Copy and complete the table below. Replace the numbers with your answers.

Organism	Habitat	Adaptation	Reasons for adaptations
Polar bear	Arctic	White fur	Keeps it camouflaged and warm
Seal	Arctic	Black coat Layer of fat	1 2
Wading bird e.g. curlew	Mud flats	Wide feet Pointed beak Long legs	3 4 5
Reptile e.g. lizard	Desert	Lives underground during the day	6
Primrose	Woodland	Flowers with brightly coloured petals and nectar	7

Destroying habitats

If habitats are destroyed, then food chains can be disrupted and in the end some species can become extinct. Human activity can destroy habitats in different ways.

- Building roads and bigger towns destroys areas of countryside and new developments cause noise and pollution.

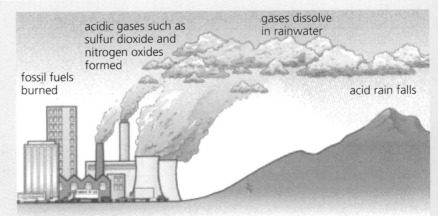

acidic gases such as sulfur dioxide and nitrogen oxides formed

gases dissolve in rainwater

fossil fuels burned

acid rain falls

- Factories, power stations and cars create a lot of gases such as sulfur dioxide which cause air pollution. These gases produce **acid rain** which can poison trees and lakes.

- Gases such as carbon dioxide which increase the **greenhouse effect** are also produced, making the Earth's atmosphere warmer and changing climates, which can threaten habitats.

Some industries dump waste into rivers and seas. **Toxic** substances, such as pesticides like DDT and some metals like mercury, can be passed through food chains. They build up in animals and poison them.

b Explain how toxic substances can build up in food chains.

Toxic substances are passed on through the food chain.

Protecting and sustaining the environment

It is important to protect all organisms and their habitats. There are many ways humans can try to do this:

- Sampling different habitats allows scientists to find out what lives there and which species may become endangered, so they can be protected.

- For each development, people should consider the needs of the environment and balance them against the human needs for food, products and services.

- People need to learn to use fewer resources, such as energy and material, or to use renewable sources of energy.

- We should recycle as many resources as possible, such as glass and plastic, and make compost so that **decomposers** (bacteria and fungi) can recycle the dead matter from plants and animals.

- Regulations can be used to limit air and water pollution, such as international agreements on greenhouse gases.

- People need to be educated about the importance of protecting the environment.

Questions

1. Make a list of all the key words on this spread with their meanings.

2. Give three ways in which a frog is adapted to its environment.

3. Give four ways in which a fox is adapted to its way of life.

4. List four things you do to protect the environment. Explain why you do each one.

5. Draw a memory map to help you remember the information about adaptation and the environment.

7.1 Biology example questions

The example questions show you how to write good answers to make sure you always get all the marks available.

The main reasons why pupils do not do as well as they think they should is that they give answers that are too general, or that are incomplete and do not give a full answer to the question.

Do not fall into this trap. Read these extra comments round the questions for useful tips that will help you get all the marks and make sure you are successful in your KS3 Test.

2 The diagram shows a plant cell.

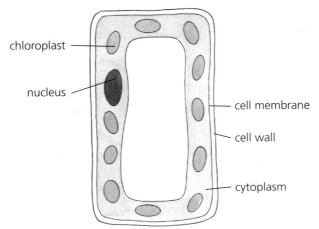

chloroplast

nucleus

cell membrane

cell wall

cytoplasm

a The cell is called a palisade cell. It makes up the tissue under the upper surface of the leaf. This is one of several types of cell you need to know about and to recognise in diagrams.

a Where in the plant would you find this type of cell? (1)

In the leaf ✓

b Most animal and plant cells have a nucleus. Give two other parts, labelled on the diagram, which are present in both animal and plant cells. (2)

Part 1 Cell membrane ✓

Part 2 Cytoplasm ✓

b Remember, plant cells have chloroplasts, a cell wall and a large vacuole, which animal cells don't.

c i What is the function of the cell wall? (1)

To give shape to the cell ✓

ii What is the function of the chloroplasts? (1)

Photosynthesis occurs in the chloroplasts.
Carbon dioxide and water are converted into glucose and oxygen ✓

Total (5)

c i The cell wall is made of cellulose. It provides support for the plant cell. Cell walls do not hold the cell contents together – this is the function of the cell membrane. Cell walls allow plant cells to stack together to make the plant.

c ii 'Photosynthesis' is the word that will get you the mark. Do not write 'to make food for the plant', as this is too vague.

Light is absorbed by the chlorophyll in the chloroplasts. This provides the energy for the photosynthesis reaction.

4 Ben copied the following information from the labels of two packets of food.

Food	Energy in kJ/100 g	Protein in g/100 g	Fat in g/100 g	Sugar in g/100 g	Fibre in g/100 g	Vitamin C in mg/100 g
X	424	6.9	0.6	3.6	6.2	0
Y	736	20.2	10.6	0	0	0

a Food Y contains a smaller variety of nutrients than food X.
Give **two** reasons why food Y might be chosen instead of food X as part of a balanced diet.   (2)
Reason 1
The rest of the person's diet might be low in protein ✓
Reason 2
The person could be underweight or ill and need a high energy intake to build them up ✓

b Ben made a curry. The label on the curry power showed:

	Calcium in mg/100 g	Iron in mg/100 g	Vitamin C in mg/100 g
curry powder	640	58.3	0

i Give one reason why calcium is needed by the body.   (1)
For healthy bones ✓
ii Give one reason why iron is needed by the body.   (1)
To make red blood cells ✓

c With his curry, Ben also had:
boiled rice; chopped-up, boiled egg;
a glass of water; a slice of lemon.
Which one of these foods provided Ben with vitamin C?   (1)
Lemon ✓

Total (5)

a The question 'Why choose food Y?' requires reasons or explanation to be given.
You need to make comparisons between food X and food Y in order to give reasons why you would choose Y. Just stating 'Food Y is much higher in energy, protein and fat' is a poor answer.

b i 'Strong *or* healthy bones *or* teeth' is a good, complete answer.
Writing the word 'bones' or 'teeth' would probably get you the mark, but the question asks for a reason.

b ii Iron is needed to make the haemoglobin in red blood cells. If you do not have enough iron you become anaemic.
Do not write just 'blood' or 'blood cells' – this does not give enough detail to get you the mark.

c Vitamin C comes from fruit, particularly citrus fruit such as lemons and oranges.

8.1 Physical changes

States of matter

Everything around us is made of **matter**. There are three **states of matter**: **solid**, **liquid** and **gas**. Each state has different properties.

a Make a table like this and list in it all the properties of each state of matter.

Solid	Liquid	Gas

solid

liquid

gas

♦ Solids are hard, dense, have a fixed volume and fixed shape, cannot be squashed and are difficult to stir.

♦ Liquids are runny, have a fixed volume, change shape to fill the bottom of their container, cannot be squashed, are easy to stir and can flow and be poured.

♦ Gases are not very dense, change volume and shape to fill all of their container, are easy to squash and can flow from place to place.

Made from particles

Everything is made from tiny **particles**. The reason why solids, liquids and gases behave in different ways is because their particles are arranged differently.

solid

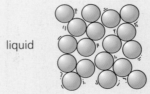
liquid

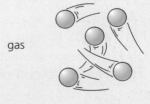
gas

♦ In a solid the particles are very close together. They are held together quite strongly in a regular pattern. Solids are usually dense because there are a lot of particles in a small volume. Because the particles are close together, a solid cannot be squashed easily.

♦ In a liquid the particles are very close together. The particles are not held together as strongly as they are in a solid. They can slide over each other and change position. Liquids are usually quite dense as there are a lot of particles in a small volume. Because the particles are close together, a liquid cannot be squashed easily.

♦ In a gas, the particles are very far apart. The particles are not held together, so they move quickly and randomly in all different directions. Gases have a low density, as there are not many particles in a small volume. Because the particles are far apart, a gas can be squashed easily.

b Draw labelled diagrams to show how the particles are arranged in a solid, a liquid and a gas.

Changing state

♦ **Melting** happens when a solid turns into a liquid at a certain temperature called the **melting point**. The melting solid takes in energy.

♦ **Boiling** happens when a liquid turns into a gas at a certain temperature called the **boiling point**. The boiling liquid takes in energy.

♦ **Freezing** happens when a liquid turns into a solid at the melting point. The freezing liquid gives out energy.

♦ **Condensing** happens when a gas turns into a liquid at the boiling point. The condensing gas gives out energy.

♦ **Evaporation** happens when a liquid turns into a gas at any temperature. An evaporating liquid takes in energy.

c Make a list of changes of state in which the particles:

   i take in energy **ii** give out energy.

Changes of state are explained further in the next spread.

Remember:

Boiling takes place throughout the liquid. Evaporation only happens at the surface of the liquid.

In every change of state mass is conserved. The mass of substance is the same before and after the change of state.

Changes of state are physical changes. They are reversible changes. No new substances are formed.

Melting point and boiling point

Every substance has a specific temperature at which it melts. This is called its **melting point**. This is also the same temperature at which it freezes.

Every substance has a specific temperature at which it boils. This is called its **boiling point**. This is also the same temperature at which it condenses.

d Look at the bar chart. Make a table with three columns headed 'Solid', 'Liquid' and 'Gas'. Put each chemical in the correct column to show its state at room temperature.

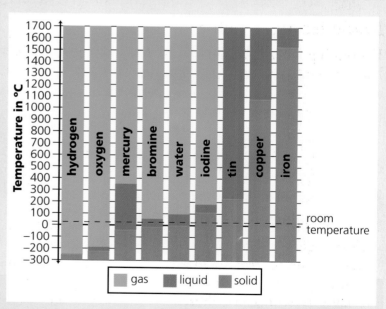

Questions

1. Make a list of all the key words on this spread with their meanings.

2. Give three ways in which a solid and liquid are different. Give three ways in which they are similar.

3. Write two sentences to explain why a liquid is more dense than a gas.

4. Write two sentences to explain why a solid is hard to squash but a gas is not.

5. Give two ways in which evaporation and boiling are different and two ways in which they are similar.

6. Draw a memory map to help you remember the information about states of matter and changes of state.

The particle model

Melting

♦ As a solid is warmed up, the heat energy makes the particles vibrate faster. The temperature rises.

♦ Once the temperature reaches the **melting point**, all the particles are vibrating so much that they overcome the pulling forces between them. The temperature stays the same while the solid melts.

♦ When all the solid has become a liquid, the temperature starts to rise again.

Boiling

♦ As a liquid is warmed up, the thermal energy makes the particles vibrate and roll over each other faster.

♦ When the temperature reaches the **boiling point**, all the particles are moving so much that they break the pulling forces between them and move away in all directions. The temperature stays the same while the liquid boils.

♦ When all the liquid has become a gas, the temperature starts to rise again.

Evaporating

♦ At the surface of the liquid, some particles gain enough energy to break away from all the others and leave the liquid behind.

♦ The particles break away as a gas. Some of the liquid has **evaporated**.

♦ Evaporation takes place at any temperature, and only at the surface of the liquid.

Condensing

♦ If a gas is cooled down, the particles lose energy and move more slowly.

♦ At the **boiling point**, some of the particles get close enough to each other to form pulling forces between them. The temperature stays the same while the gas condenses.

♦ When all the gas has become a liquid, the temperature starts to fall again.

Freezing

♦ If a liquid is cooled down, the particles lose energy and move more slowly.

♦ At the **melting point** they are just vibrating back and forth. Stronger pulling forces form between the particles and they make a regular arrangement. The temperature stays the same while the liquid freezes.

♦ When all the liquid has become a solid, the temperature starts to fall again.

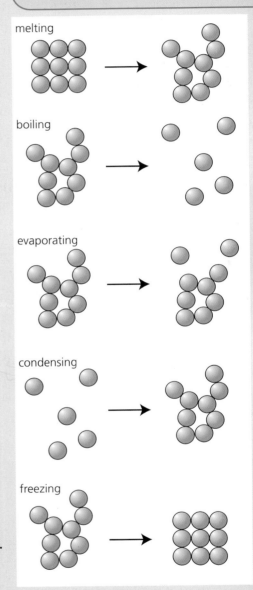

melting

boiling

evaporating

condensing

freezing

a What happens to the pulling forces between the particles as ice melts and as water boils?

b What happens to the pulling forces between the particles as a gas condenses and as a liquid freezes?

Diffusion

Diffusion happens in gases and liquids when particles spread out and mix with other particles, for example, when the smell of a perfume spreads through the air. The particles move away from their source (the perfume bottle) and mix with the air particles. The smell gets weaker as the particles move further and further apart. They move to fill all the available space evenly.

Diffusion is faster in hot gases or liquids because the particles are moving faster.

Gas pressure

The gas particles inside this balloon are moving in all directions and constantly hitting the rubber. Every time a particle hits the rubber, it gives it a tiny push. This keeps the balloon in shape. The sum of all these forces on the area of the balloon is called **gas pressure**.

Expansion and contraction

An increase in temperature makes the particles in matter move more. They take up more space, so the matter **expands**. A decrease in temperature makes the particles move less. They take up less space, so the matter **contracts**.

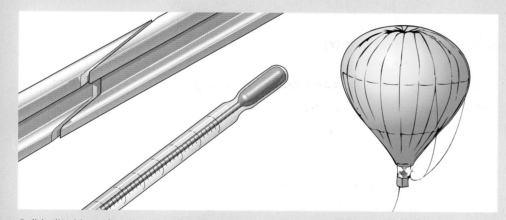

Solids, liquids and gases expand and contract.

c Write two sentences to explain why, at first, the smell of a stink bomb is stronger close to where it was let off than at the other side of the room.

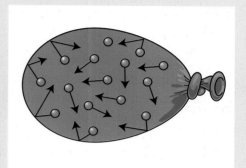

Remember:
The particles themselves do not change size.

Gases expand and contract more than liquids and solids.

d Draw diagrams showing the particles before and after you heat:
  i a solid
  ii a liquid
  iii a gas in a balloon.

Questions

1. Make a list of all the key words on this spread with their meanings.

2. Write two sentences to explain what happens to the arrangement of the particles when a gas condenses to a liquid.

3. Write two sentences to explain what happens to the arrangement of the particles when a liquid freezes to a solid.

4. Explain to John how solids, liquids and gases can expand or contract without the particles changing size.

5. Explain why power cables seem to have more slack on a hot day than on a cold day.

6. Draw a memory map to help you remember how the particle model can explain changes of state, diffusion, gas pressure and expansion and contraction.

8.3 Elements, mixtures and compounds

What are substances made of?

- **Atoms** are the smallest particles in an element.
- An **element** is made up of only one type of atom. Examples of elements include copper, iron, oxygen, hydrogen, sulfur, mercury and zinc.
- A **compound** is a substance that is made up of more than one type of atom chemically joined together. Examples of compounds include water, hydrogen sulfide and sodium chloride.
- A **mixture** contains more than one element or compound which are just physically mixed together. They are not chemically joined. Examples of mixtures include air and sea water.

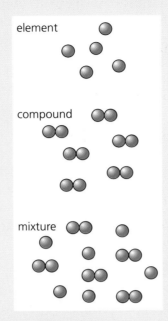

element

compound

mixture

a Write two sentences to describe the difference between an element and a compound.

b Which of these substances are elements and which are compounds?

water   iron   sugar oxygen   carbon dioxide hydrogen

Dissolving

- Some chemicals **dissolve**. They are **soluble**. Other chemicals do not dissolve. They are **insoluble**.
- The substance that dissolves is called the **solute**. The liquid that it dissolves in is called the **solvent**. The mixture of solute dissolved in solvent is called a **solution**.
- When no more can dissolve, the solution is **saturated**. The amount of a chemical that can dissolve in a solvent is called its **solubility**.
- The mass of solution is the same as the mass of solvent + solute. Mass is conserved when you make a solution.

When a solid dissolves in water, the solvent particles surround the particles of the solid. The solid crystal is broken up. To make the solute dissolve faster you can do the following:

- Use hotter solvent. The solvent particles have more energy and are moving around more.
- Stir it. The particles move around more.
- Grind the solute into a powder. More solute particles will be in contact with the solvent.

c Is dissolving a physical or chemical change?

d Monica wants to dissolve some sugar as fast as possible. Give three things she can do to speed it up.

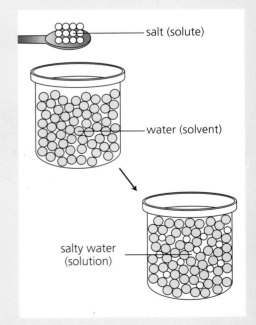

salt (solute)

water (solvent)

salty water (solution)

Remember: if you evaporate the solvent away, you get back the solute that you dissolved. This shows that mass is conserved, and that dissolving is reversible.

Separating mixtures

Mixtures are made of substances that are not chemically joined together. They can be separated using different techniques. These work because the physical properties of the elements or compounds in the mixture are different.

Chromatography is used to separate a mixture of coloured compounds.

♦ The mixture is put onto a piece of filter paper and then dipped into a solvent.

♦ As the solvent moves up the paper, it carries the chemicals up with it.

♦ If a chemical is very soluble, it moves a long way.

♦ If a chemical is not very soluble, it moves only a short way.

e Why is it possible to separate the different chemicals in a mixture?

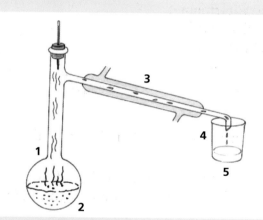

ink **A**   ink **B**   ink **C**   ink **D**

Distillation is used to purify liquids by separating the liquid from any solids that are dissolved in it.

1 The salty water is heated until it boils. The water turns into a gas, called **water vapour**, and rises up the flask.

2 The salt starts to form crystals at the bottom of the flask.

3 In the condenser the water vapour is cooled and it condenses back into liquid water.

4 The water drips into the beaker.

5 This water is **pure**. It has no other substances in it. We call it **distilled water**.

f Copy the flow chart below about distillation. Under each box, add a label to show whether the water particles gain or lose energy at each stage.

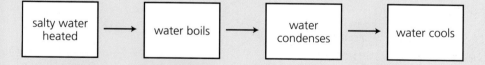

Questions

1. Make a list of all the key words on this spread with their meanings.

2. Crystallisation is the reverse of dissolving. Is crystallisation a chemical change or a physical change?

3. What type of change is:
   a freezing water?   b frying an egg?
   c baking clay?

4. What process would you use to separate:
   a sand from pebbles?
   b five different coloured inks?
   c a muddy sample of salt to get pure salt?

5. Draw a memory map to help you remember the information about elements, compounds, dissolving and separating mixtures.

Rocks

The Earth's surface

Rocks form the surface **crust** of the Earth. Rocks are made from a mixture of different chemicals. These chemicals are called **minerals**.

Physical weathering

Physical weathering happens when rock is broken into smaller pieces, but not changed into new substances. It is a physical change. It can be caused by the effect of wind, water and changes in temperature. These types of weathering are very common in mountains and desert regions.

- **Freeze-thaw**: water can get into cracks in the rock. If this water freezes it expands, making the crack bigger.
- **Heating and cooling**: rocks get hot during the day and expand. They get cold at night and contract. This leads to cracking.
- **Wind**: fine grains of sand are carried by the wind and blown against the surface of the rock so they gradually wear it away.

Chemical weathering

Chemical weathering happens when chemicals in the air and water react with the compounds in the rock to make new substances. It is a chemical change.

- Rainwater is slightly acidic because there is carbon dioxide dissolved in it. Rainwater may also be more acidic because of pollution. Then it is called **acid rain**.
- Many statues and buildings are made of a rock called limestone (calcium carbonate).
- When acidic rain falls on limestone, it reacts with it and produces a new chemical. This new chemical is soluble and dissolves.

Erosion

Erosion happens when rocks are weathered and the pieces are carried away. Erosion can be caused by wind, water and glaciers.

Types of rock

The table on the next page summarises the three types of rock.

c Give two features that would help you identify a sedimentary rock.

d Give two features that would help you identify a metamorphic rock.

Remember:
You must know the difference between physical and chemical weathering.

In physical weathering, no new substances are formed.

In chemical weathering, new substances are formed.

a What is the result of physical weathering?

b What is the result of chemical weathering?

Remember:
Weathering + transport = erosion

Remember: the oldest sedimentary layers are at the bottom.

Type of rock	Description	Examples
Igneous	Formed from molten rock, called **magma**, which has cooled and solidified. Sometimes it comes out of volcanoes or cracks in the Earth's crust. Sometimes it solidifies below ground. Igneous rock contains crystals. The bigger the crystals, the slower it cooled. Igneous rocks do not react with acid.	Basalt (small crystals) Granite (big crystals)
Sedimentary	Formed from layers of **sediment** that settle at the bottoms of rivers, lakes and seas over millions of years. The layers are squashed by the weight of the layers above them. The **grains** of sediment are different sizes and become stuck together to form rock. Dead animals and plants are covered by sediment and become **fossils**. Limestone and chalk react with acid, but sandstone and mudstone do not.	Limestone Sandstone Mudstone Chalk
Metamorphic	Formed from sedimentary or igneous rocks that have been exposed to high pressure and/or high temperature. This causes changes in the rocks over a very long period of time. Metamorphic rocks may have layers or tiny crystals in them. Fossils are usually destroyed by the heat and pressure. Marble reacts with acid, but slate does not.	Marble (made from limestone) Slate (made from mudstone)

The rock cycle

The **rock cycle** is a continuous cycle of changing rock from igneous rock to sedimentary, to metamorphic and back to igneous rock. This cycle can take many millions of years to complete.

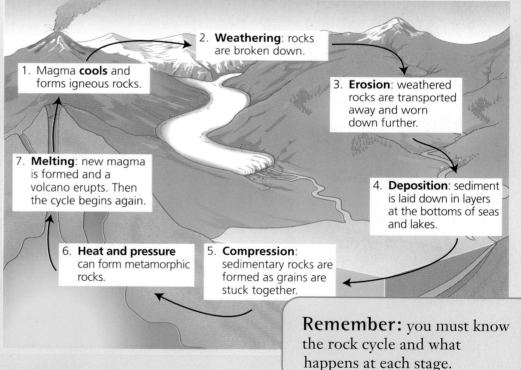

1. Magma **cools** and forms igneous rocks.

2. **Weathering**: rocks are broken down.

3. **Erosion**: weathered rocks are transported away and worn down further.

4. **Deposition**: sediment is laid down in layers at the bottoms of seas and lakes.

5. **Compression**: sedimentary rocks are formed as grains are stuck together.

6. **Heat and pressure** can form metamorphic rocks.

7. **Melting**: new magma is formed and a volcano erupts. Then the cycle begins again.

> **Remember**: you must know the rock cycle and what happens at each stage.

Questions

1. Make a list of all the key words on this spread with their meanings.

2. Explain the difference between physical weathering and chemical weathering.

3. Explain why basalt and granite have different sized crystals.

4. Write a rhyme to help you remember the stages in the rock cycle.

5. Draw a memory map to help you remember information about types of weathering, different rock types and the rock cycle.

8.5 Chemical changes

Reactants and products

In a chemical change, new substances are formed. The atoms in the **reactants** are rearranged to form new substances, the **products**. Mass is conserved.

There are many different chemical reactions that you need to know. They are summarised here.

Remember: in a chemical change, reactants react and produce products.

reactants → products

Reacting with oxygen

Oxygen may react with a substance and produce an oxide. Some **non-metals react with oxygen**:

carbon + oxygen → carbon dioxide

hydrogen + oxygen → water (hydrogen oxide)

Some **metals react with oxygen**. The general equation is:

metal + oxygen → metal oxide

For example,

magnesium + oxygen → magnesium oxide

The **combustion of a fuel** is a reaction with oxygen. The general equation is:

hydrocarbon + oxygen → carbon dioxide + water

For example,

methane + oxygen → carbon dioxide + water

a Copy and complete the word equations.

i calcium + oxygen →

ii zinc + oxygen →

Neutralisation of acids

You can **neutralise** an **acid** to form a **salt**. Different chemicals will neutralise acids, such as alkalis, metals, metal oxides and metal carbonates.

You can **neutralise an acid with an alkali**. The general equation is:

acid + alkali → salt + water

For example,

hydrochloric acid + sodium hydroxide → sodium chloride + water

You can **neutralise an acid with some metals**. The general equation is:

acid + metal → salt + hydrogen

For example,

hydrochloric acid + zinc → zinc chloride + hydrogen

Remember:
Hydrochloric acid makes chloride salts.
Sulfuric acid makes sulfate salts.
Nitric acid makes nitrate salts.

Remember:
Both alkalis and metal oxides are bases.
The general equation is:
acid + base → salt + water

You can **neutralise an acid with some metal oxides**.
The general equation is:
    acid + metal oxide → salt + water

For example,
    hydrochloric acid + magnesium oxide → magnesium chloride + water

You can **neutralise an acid with a metal carbonate**. The general equation is:
    acid + carbonate → salt + water + carbon dioxide

For example,
    hydrochloric acid + calcium carbonate → calcium chloride + water + carbon dioxide

b Copy and complete the word equations.

   i nitric acid + sodium hydroxide →

   ii sulfuric acid + calcium carbonate →

Questions

1. Make a list of all the key words on this spread with their meanings.

2. Write word equations for three substances reacting with oxygen.

3. Copy and complete the following general word equations for neutralisation reactions:
    a acid + alkali →
    b acid + metal →
    c acid + metal oxide →

4. Draw a memory map to help you remember the information about reactions with oxygen and neutralisation reactions.

Chemistry example questions

a These terms are ones you need to remember.

Remember that water melts and freezes at its melting point.

Water boils and condenses at its boiling point.

b Look at the graph.

① The ice starts to melt after about 6 minutes.

② The temperature does not start to go up until all the ice has melted at 0 °C.

c You will get two marks for each drawing. The ticks show what you will get the marks for.

Remember to draw circles at the size indicated. Try to draw them roughly the same size. You will lose a mark if they are of very different sizes.

The particles in solids are regularly arranged and close packed. The circles can alternate rather than lining up, e.g.

The particles in liquids are random or irregular, but close packed. You cannot squeeze a liquid into a smaller volume. In your drawings make sure there are not too many spaces and that each circle touches at least two other circles.

Gases are mainly empty space with particles racing about and bouncing off each other. Show no more than three circles in your drawing.

3 Water can exist in three physical states: ice, water and steam.

a What is the name given to the process that changes: (2)

   i ice into water?   _melting_ ✓

   ii steam into water?   _condensing_ ✓

b A beaker of ice was placed in a warm room. The graph shows how the temperature in the beaker changed from the start of the experiment.

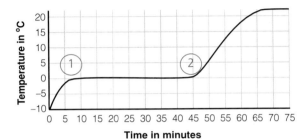

How long after the start had all the ice just gone? (1)

   _45_ minutes

c Draw diagrams, in the boxes below, to show the arrangement of water molecules in ice, water and steam. Use circles, like this ◯, to represent the water molecules.

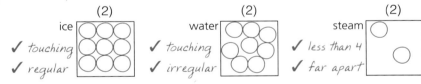

d Water is a compound of two elements. A diagram of a water molecule is shown below. In this diagram the circles represent atoms.

In the circles, write the correct symbols for the elements. (1)

Total (10)

d The formula for water is H_2O. If you think about the number of atoms here, the two smaller circles must be Hs for hydrogen and the larger one must be O for oxygen. You are not expected to remember this shape but you ought to be able to think out the answer.

5 Alex has four solids. They are labelled **W, X, Y** and **Z**. He adds a sample of each one to some dilute acid. The table shows his results.

Solid	Result with dilute acid
W	it reacts slowly and gives off hydrogen
X	it reacts quickly and gives off carbon dioxide
Y	it dissolves and the liquid becomes warm
Z	it remains undissolved as a white powder

a i Which solid could be chalk (calcium carbonate)?   (1)

X ✓

ii Give the name of another rock which reacts with acid in the same way as chalk.   (1)

Limestone ✓

b i One of the solids is a metal. State which one and give the reason for your choice.   (2)

W because it gives off hydrogen with acid ✓

ii The list below gives five metals.

copper   gold   potassium   sodium   zinc

Write them in order of reactivity starting with the most reactive.   (1)

Most reactive Potassium Sodium Zinc

Copper Gold Least reactive ✓

iii Give the name of another metal which would react with acid in a similar way to zinc.   (1)

Iron ✓

c As each of the solids reacts, the acid is used up. Describe a test you can use to show whether or not acid is still present.   (2)

Add universal indicator. ✓ *It turns from green to red if acid is present. It stays green if the acid has been used up.* ✓

Total (8)

a i All carbonates react with acid to give carbon dioxide.

a ii Chalk and limestone are sedimentary rocks made of calcium carbonate. Marble is another correct answer. Marble is a metamorphic rock made of calcium carbonate.

b i With acid, reactive metals give off hydrogen. They react to form the metal salt. The more reactive they are, the faster they react.

b ii You need to know a reactivity series, e.g.

potassium
sodium
calcium
magnesium
aluminium
zinc
iron
[hydrogen]
copper
silver
gold

Notice hydrogen is in the series to link it with reactions with acids. A metal above hydrogen will react with acids to give hydrogen gas. A metal below hydrogen will not.

c To get the second mark you need to show the result of the test if the acid is still present, as well as the result if the acid is used up.

Writing 'Use indicator' would not get you a mark unless it was obvious from the colour changes you gave which indicator you meant.

b iii If you know your reactivity series, questions like this are very easy. The metal just above or just below zinc will react in a similar way. Metals above aluminium will react much more quickly, and metals below iron will not react.

9.1 Energy resources

Non-renewable energy resources

Non-renewable energy resources are not replaced as we use them. These resources will run out in the future. We will need to find other energy resources to use instead.

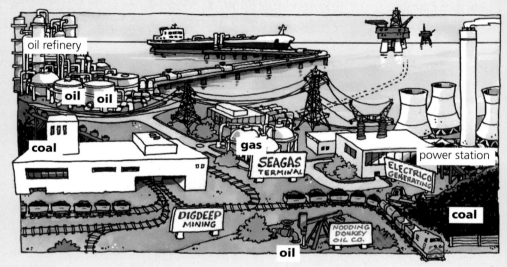

Fossil fuels

Coal, oil and gas are **fossil fuels**. They are non-renewable because they are formed by a process that takes millions of years:

♦ Animals and plants die.
♦ They are buried under layers of sediment.
♦ There is little oxygen, so they rot very slowly.
♦ They are heated and put under pressure.
♦ Over millions of years the plants turn into coal and the animals turn into crude oil and natural gas.

> **Remember:** the energy from fossil fuels originally came from the Sun.

Pollution

Fossil fuels can be burned in power stations to generate electricity, or in vehicles to provide energy to move around. Burning fossil fuels produces gases, mainly carbon dioxide along with other gases. These gases can cause **pollution** problems. These include:

♦ **acid rain**: some gases, such as sulfur dioxide, dissolve in rain and make an acidic solution.
♦ **global warming**: some gases, such as carbon dioxide, keep the heat in, and cause the temperature to rise on the Earth. This changes the climate.
♦ **smog**: this is a mixture of polluting gases and soot, which collects over cities and can cause breathing difficulties.

a Give two disadvantages of fossil fuels.

b Make a flow chart to show how fossil fuels are formed.

Alternative energy resources

We need to use alternatives to fossil fuels. Many of these **alternative energy resources** are **renewable**, which means they are replaced as we use them.

Biomass such as wood or other crops can be burned for heating. Methane can be burned for heating or in vehicles, or used to generate electricity. Ethanol can be burned in vehicles.

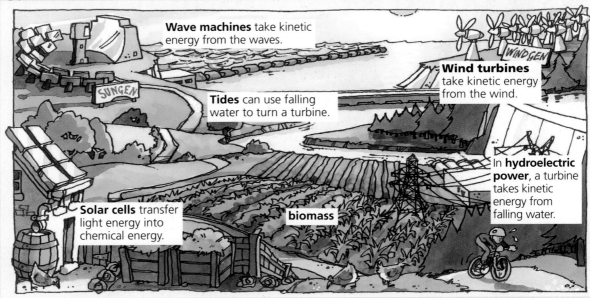

Wave machines take kinetic energy from the waves.

Wind turbines take kinetic energy from the wind.

Tides can use falling water to turn a turbine.

In **hydroelectric power**, a turbine takes kinetic energy from falling water.

Solar cells transfer light energy into chemical energy.

biomass

Batteries store chemical energy, which can be used to power vehicles.

The picture shows some alternative energy resources that can be used to generate electricity.

Less polluting

Renewable energy resources do not produce as many polluting gases as burning fossil fuels. However, some people feel that alternative energy resources cause other forms of pollution, such as:

♦ wind turbines produce noise pollution

♦ tidal barriers and hydroelectric power stations in the mountains disturb the environment as land is flooded and habitats are changed.

Remember: the energy from all these renewable sources (except tides) originally came from the Sun.

c Give two advantages of using renewable energy resources.

Questions

1. Make a list of all the key words on this spread with their meanings.

2. Make a table with two headings, 'Renewable' and 'Non-renewable'. Put the energy resources on this spread into your table.

3. Explain why all energy resources, except tidal energy, come from the Sun originally.

4. List three pollution problems caused by fossil fuels. Then write two sentences to explain each one.

5. Draw a memory map to help you remember the information about non-renewable and renewable energy resources and pollution.

Electricity and magnetism

Symbols

Drawing lamps, batteries and switches takes a long time. It is easier to draw circuits using **circuit symbols** to represent the parts.

batteries   lamp   switch

Circuits

Electricity transfers energy to make things work. You need a complete **circuit** for electricity to flow. If there are any gaps then the electricity will not be able to go around the circuit. The diagram shows a simple circuit with a single battery, a lamp and a switch.

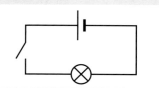

a Draw a circuit with two batteries, two lamps and one switch.

Measuring current

Current is measured in **amps**, **A**, using an **ammeter**. The ammeter is put in the circuit. The circuit symbol for an ammeter is Ⓐ

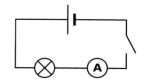

♦ The current is the same on both sides of the lamp.

♦ Increasing the number of batteries increases the current and the lamp is brighter.

♦ Decreasing the number of batteries decreases the current and the lamp is dimmer.

♦ Increasing the number of lamps decreases the current and the lamps are dimmer.

♦ Decreasing the number of lamps increases the current and the lamps are brighter.

b You have a circuit with a lamp and two batteries. What happens to the lamp after one battery is removed?

c You have a circuit with a battery and two lamps. What happens to one lamp after the other lamp is removed?

Measuring voltage

Voltage is measured in **volts**, **V**, using a **voltmeter**. Voltage is measured across any part of the circuit. The circuit symbol for a voltmeter is Ⓥ

There is a voltage across any part of a circuit where energy goes into the circuit or leaves the circuit. For example, there is a voltage across a lamp or a battery, but not across wires. You can increase the voltage in a circuit by adding more batteries.

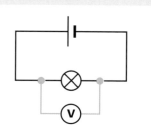

Series and parallel

In a **series circuit**:

♦ The lamps are side by side.

♦ If one lamp goes out, they will all go out.

♦ The current is the same all the way around the circuit.

♦ The voltage is shared between the lamps.

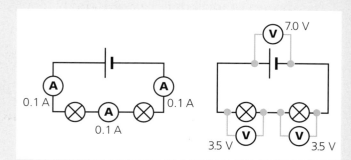

In a **parallel circuit**:

♦ The lamps are in different loops.

♦ If one lamp goes out, the rest will stay on.

♦ The current is shared between the loops.

♦ The voltage is the same across the battery and each lamp.

d Make a table with the headings 'Series' and 'Parallel'. Fill in the table to compare the voltage, current and lamp brightness in each type of circuit.

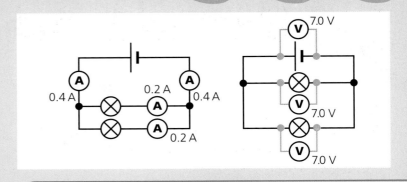

Remember: lamps in parallel are brighter than the same lamps in series using the same battery.

Magnets

A magnet produces a **magnetic field**. Magnetic fields can be shown by drawing **magnetic field lines**. These lines run from the **north pole** to the **south pole** of the magnet.

Unlike magnetic poles **attract**.
Like magnetic poles **repel**.

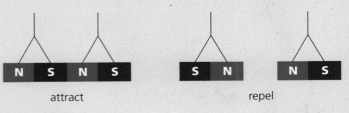

Iron, nickel and cobalt are magnetic metals.

Electromagnets

An **electromagnet** is a coil of wire with an electric current running through it. It acts like a magnet. If the coil has an iron core inside, it makes the magnet stronger. Electromagnets can be used in scrap metal yards for picking up cars.

Questions

1. Make a list of all the key words on this spread with their meanings.

2. Give three ways in which a series circuit and a parallel circuit are different.

3. You have been given two lamps and three switches. Design a circuit that will let you switch off the lamps together and also separately.

4. The magnetic field around a bar magnet and an electromagnet are the same. Draw a diagram showing the magnetic field lines around an electromagnet.

5. Draw a memory map to help you remember all the information about electric circuits, magnets and electromagnetism.

Light

- ◆ Light travels away from its **source** in straight lines in all directions.
- ◆ Light travels at a speed of 300 million metres per second in air.
- ◆ We see when light enters our eyes.
- ◆ Shadows are formed when the light is blocked.

Reflection

- ◆ When light hits a smooth surface, such as a mirror, it is **reflected**.
- ◆ The **incoming ray** hits the mirror and is reflected. It is then called the **reflected ray**.
- ◆ The angle between the ray and the surface is the same for the incoming ray and the reflected ray. This is the **law of reflection**.
- ◆ When the surface is not smooth, such as paper, the light hits the surface and becomes **scattered**. In this case the light comes in from one direction but is reflected in many different directions.
- ◆ Some surfaces **absorb** the light and little or no light is reflected back. Dark surfaces absorb more light, while pale surfaces absorb less light.

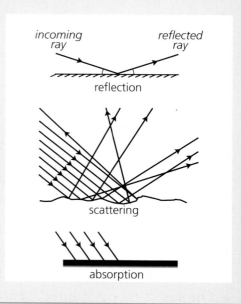

a Copy and complete the table.

Scientific word	Meaning
Reflection	
Scattering	
Absorption	

Remember:
You must know the difference between the reflection and the scattering of light.
When you draw ray diagrams you must draw the light rays with a ruler and show the direction of the ray with an arrow.

Refraction

Light travels through **transparent** materials but not through **opaque** materials. When light travels from one transparent material to another it may become **refracted**.

- ◆ Light bends inwards when it travels from air into glass or water.
- ◆ Light bends outwards when it travels from glass or water into air.
- ◆ If the light is travelling at 90° to the surface, it does not bend.

b Copy and complete the diagram below showing a ray of light passing from air into a glass block.

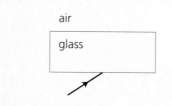

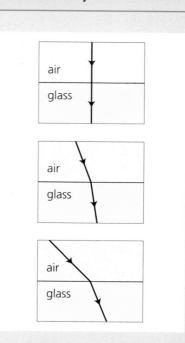

Colour

- White light is made of many colours, which can be seen when white light passes through a prism. This produces a **spectrum**.
- This splitting up of light into its colours is known as **dispersion.**
- The colours are always refracted in the same order: red, orange, yellow, green, blue, indigo and violet.

c Draw a diagram showing white light being dispersed by a prism.

> **Remember:** the spectrum by using the mnemonic ROY G BIV.

Sound

- A sound is made when something **vibrates**.
- We hear sound because vibrations travel through the air to our ears and make the eardrum vibrate.
- Sounds cannot travel through a vacuum because sound needs a material to travel through.

Loudness and amplitude

- The **amplitude** is the height of the vibration from the centre.
- Amplitude can be measured in metres.
- The larger the amplitude of a vibration, the louder the sound.
- The smaller the amplitude of a vibration, the quieter the sound.
- Loud sounds transfer a lot of energy and can damage your hearing.

d Explain how sounds can damage your hearing.

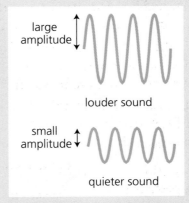

Sound and light

- Both light and sound transfer energy.
- Light and sound can be reflected. Reflected sound is called an **echo**.
- Both light and sound travel at different speeds in different materials.
- Light travels at 300 million m/s, much faster than sound which travels at 330 m/s. Thunder and lightning show that sound and light travel at different speeds.

e Make a list of three things that sound and light have in common.

Questions

1. Make a list of all the key words on this spread with their meanings.

2. Explain how sounds travels down a string telephone (two tins attached by a string).

3. Explain the difference between reflection of light and refraction of light.

4. Draw a diagram to show an oscilloscope screen showing a vibration that gives:
   a a quiet sound　　**b** a loud sound.

5. Draw two overlapping memory maps, one for light and one for sound. In the overlap will be all the things that sound and light have in common.

Forces and motion

Forces in action

The effects of forces can be seen everywhere. When you push or pull an object you are using a force.

Different types of force include:

♦ weight ♦ friction ♦ tension ♦ upthrust ♦ reaction force.

weight of Flo

Weight

♦ **Weight** is the force of **gravity** on an object and like all forces it is measured in **newtons** (N).

♦ Weight or **gravitational force** pulls an object towards a large object, usually the Earth.

♦ The further apart two objects are, the smaller the force between them.

♦ The gravitational force of an object also depends on its mass.

a Explain the difference between mass and weight.

> **Remember:** weight is a force. It should not be confused with mass, which is a measure of how much matter an object has, and is measured in kg.

Friction

♦ **Friction** is the force that happens when two things rub together.

♦ Friction slows moving objects down, and causes thermal energy to be given out.

♦ Friction is useful in brakes in cars and bicycles.

♦ Friction can cause problems by wearing down machinery.

♦ Friction can be reduced by using **lubricants**.

♦ **Air resistance** is an example of friction, which slows down moving objects.

♦ Cars and planes are **streamlined** to keep their air resistance low.

friction   force of engine

b Explain how friction and air resistance can be reduced.

Unbalanced and balanced forces

Unbalanced forces:

♦ When forces act against each other and they are not the same size, they are **unbalanced**.

♦ If a stationary object has unbalanced forces acting on it, it will start to move in the direction of the biggest force. If you give a push to a trolley and your push is bigger than the forces acting on it, such as friction, the trolley will move in the direction of your push.

♦ If the bigger force on a moving object is in the same direction as the movement, then the object will speed up. If the bigger force is in the opposite direction to the movement, the object will slow down.

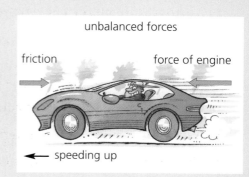

unbalanced forces

friction   force of engine

← speeding up

Balanced forces:

- ◆ If two forces are the same size and acting in opposite directions, they are **balanced**.
- ◆ A vehicle travelling at a steady speed and something standing still both have balanced forces acting on them.
- ◆ A floating object has balanced forces acting on it. The **upthrust** (the force of the water pushing up) is equal to the object's **weight** (the force acting down on the water).
- ◆ The **reaction force** stops something falling through a solid object. When a person stands on a plank, the reaction force of the plank balances the weight of the person.
- ◆ When a weight pulls down on a rope or spring, the weight is balanced by the **tension** force in the rope or spring pulling up.

c Copy and complete this table.

Balanced or unbalanced forces?	Description	Example
Balanced	Forces are the same size and act in opposite directions	i
ii	iii	A car accelerating

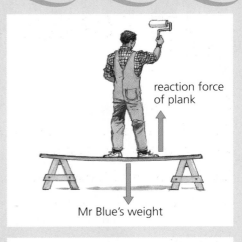

reaction force of plank

Mr Blue's weight

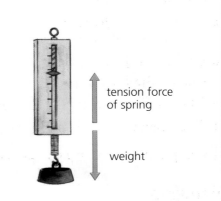

tension force of spring

weight

Speed

You can tell how fast an object is moving by measuring the distance it travels and the time it takes. **Speed** is measured in metres per second. You can calculate the speed using this equation:

$$\text{speed} = \frac{\text{distance travelled}}{\text{time taken}}$$

A speed of 100 m/s is much faster than a speed of 10 m/s.

Remember this equation.

d Louise ran 40 metres in 10 seconds. Use the equation to calculate her speed.

Questions

1. Make a list of all the key words on this spread with their meanings.

2. A car is pulling a trailer forwards. There is friction between the wheels and the road acting against the pull of the car.
   - **a** Draw a diagram to show the forces on the trailer.
     The friction is 300 N while the car pulls with a force of 500 N.
   - **b** In which direction does the trailer move?
   - **c** What is the overall or resultant force on the trailer?

3. Explain why a toy boat floating on a pond shows an example of balanced forces.

4. Draw a memory map to help you remember the information about forces and speed.

9.5 Earth and space

The Solar System

◆ The **Solar System** consists of nine **planets** and their **moons**, and also other objects such as **comets** and **asteroids**, orbiting the **Sun**.

◆ Planets orbit the Sun and moons orbit planets.

◆ The nine planets in order from the Sun are Mercury, Venus, Earth, Mars, Jupiter, Saturn, Uranus, Neptune and Pluto.

◆ The planets differ from each other in many ways, including diameter, surface temperature and distance from the Sun.

a Describe what makes up the Solar System.

The Sun and stars

◆ The Sun is a **star** and it is the source of light for the Earth.

◆ Like all stars, the Sun is **luminous** which means that it gives out light.

◆ We can only see the planets and our Moon because they reflect the light from the Sun. They are **non-luminous**.

b Write a paragraph explaining the difference between luminous and non-luminous objects.

Day and night

◆ The Earth spins on its **axis**, an imaginary line that runs between the Poles, once every 24 hours.

◆ As the Earth spins, the UK moves from shadow at night, when it faces away from the Sun, into the light during the day, when it is facing the Sun.

◆ The Sun appears to rise in the east and set in the west.

c Explain what causes day and night using the following words:

axis   shadow   Sun   Earth

night   day

light from Sun

equator

axis

The seasons

◆ The Earth orbits the Sun every 365 days. This is called a **year**. During this time in the UK there are four **seasons**: spring, summer, autumn and winter.

◆ The seasons are caused by the tilt of the Earth on its axis.

◆ The UK is in the northern hemisphere. In the summer, the UK is tilted towards the Sun, giving warmer weather. In the winter, the UK is tilted away from the Sun, giving colder weather. The diagram on the next page shows this.

- The tilt of the Earth also causes day length to vary at different times of the year. The days are longer in the summer and shorter in the winter.

- The stars we see in the night sky change with the seasons because we are facing a different way out into space.

d Describe two differences caused by the tilt of the Earth that we notice between winter and summer.

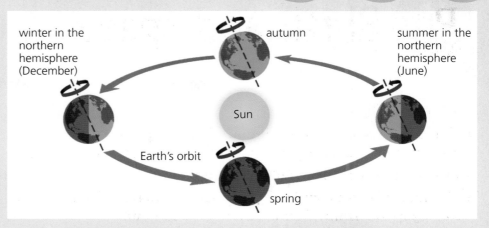

winter in the northern hemisphere (December)

autumn

summer in the northern hemisphere (June)

Sun

Earth's orbit

spring

Satellites

- A **satellite** is an object that orbits a larger object.

- The Moon is the **natural** satellite of the Earth. **Artificial** satellites are put into space by scientists.

- Artificial satellites have many uses, for example, communication, exploration, weather forecasting and navigation.

- Artificial satellites can be put into different types of orbit such as **polar** and **geostationary** orbits. Geostationary satellites orbit the Earth once every 24 hours and they stay in the same place over the Earth. Polar satellites orbit over the North and South Poles.

- The planets orbit the Sun and are satellites of the Sun.

- The planets are kept in orbit by **gravitational force** between them and the Sun. The size of this force depends on the size of the planet and its distance from the Sun.

e Give two examples of natural satellites and two examples of artificial satellites.

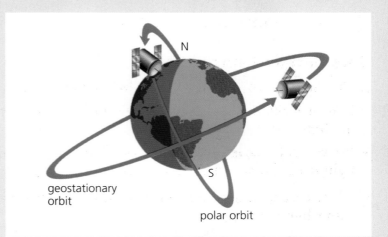

N

geostationary orbit

S

polar orbit

Questions

1. Make a list of all the key words on this spread with their meanings.

2. **a** Name the planet closest to the Sun.
   b Explain how this affects the surface temperature and length of year on this planet.

3. Draw a diagram to explain how we see the Moon.

4. Draw a memory map to help you remember the information about the Solar System, day and night, the seasons and satellites.

Physics example questions

a When choosing an answer from a list, always copy correctly and completely. Do not shorten 'reaction of the ground' to 'reaction'.

b The symbol for the unit of force is N (capital). The word is newton (without a capital letter).

c These answers always require a sentence. You need to include the link that to get faster needs a bigger forward force.

If you were unsure about the name of force B, an answer like 'The force from Jack's hand is larger than force B' is acceptable because it uses the information from the diagram.

Do not write 'It is bigger' because the marker does not know what 'it' refers to.

---

8 Jack is pushing a luggage trolley along level ground at an airport.

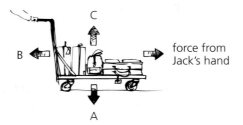

There are four forces acting on the trolley.

a One of the forces is the push from Jack's hands. The others are friction, weight and the reaction of the ground.

Complete the sentences. (3)

Force A is   *weight* ✓

Force B is   *friction* ✓

Force C is   *reaction of the ground* ✓

b What are the units in which force is measured? (1)

newtons ✓

c The trolley is moving forwards, and it is getting faster. One pair of forces is now unbalanced.
Compare the sizes of these two forces. (1)

The forward force of Jack's hand must now be bigger than the backward force of friction. ✓

d Jack has to push the trolley 150 m to the check-in desk.
If he pushes the trolley at 3 m/s, how long will it take him? (1)

$$\text{Speed} = \frac{distance}{time} \qquad 3 = \frac{150}{?}$$

$$\text{therefore } ? = \frac{150}{3} = 50\,s \checkmark$$

Total (6)

---

d In any calculation, write down the equation in the form that you remember it and put the numbers in. Then rearrange the equation. Use small numbers to help you check your rearranged equation. For example, $3 = \frac{6}{?}$ is easier to rearrange than an equation with letters involving algebra.

Many speed calculations can be done using common sense rather than the formula:

$$\text{speed} = \frac{distance}{time}$$

It always pays to check your answers using common sense. Think to yourself: if it goes 3 m in 1 second then it goes 30 m in 10 seconds or 90 m in 30 seconds. So it goes 150 m in 50 seconds. Do not forget the units!

11 a The Earth is the third planet from the Sun.

   i Which is the second planet from the Sun?   (1)

     Venus ✓

   ii Which is the fourth planet from the Sun?   (1)

     Mars ✓

b The diagram shows the orbits of the Earth and Mercury. Mercury takes 88 Earth-days to orbit the Sun.

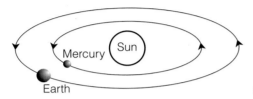

not to scale

In the diagram, the Earth and Mercury are lined up with the Sun. How long will it take before the Earth and Mercury are lined up with the Sun again? Tick the correct box.   (1)

less than 88 Earth-days   ☐

exactly 88 Earth-days   ☐

more than 88 Earth-days   ✓

exactly 365 Earth-days   ☐

c Mercury and Pluto are both small rocky planets. Mercury is one of the brightest objects in the night sky, but Pluto is so faint that it cannot be seen with the naked eye.

Give **two** reasons why Mercury is much brighter than Pluto.   (2)

Reason 1

Mercury is nearer the Sun so gets more light than Pluto ✓

Reason 2

Earth is nearer Mercury than Pluto so light has less

distance to travel after being reflected. ✓

Total (5)

a You need to remember the order of the planets in the Solar System from the Sun, at least to Jupiter: Mercury; Venus; Earth; Mars; Jupiter; Saturn; Uranus; Neptune; Pluto.

b Mercury takes 88 days to get back to the same place (where it is shown on the diagram). In this time the Earth will have moved on about one-quarter of an orbit so Mercury will have to cover at least another quarter of its orbit to catch up with Earth.

c The further light, or any form of energy, has to travel, the more the light or energy spreads out. Mercury is nearer to the Sun than Pluto. It receives much more light. Light also has less distance to travel from Mercury to Earth than from Pluto to Earth, so spreads out less. Good answers include both parts of the explanation.

Investigations using experiments (1)

Step 1: finding a question to investigate

Does sugar dissolve quicker in hot tea than in cold tea?

*You've made the first step – you have a question you want to answer. Now you have to turn it into an **investigation**. This is an investigation you can carry out in a school laboratory, by doing experiments.*

Key to understanding these spreads:

black = main text

red = 'Sid the scientist'

blue = 'Pippa the pupil'

Step 2: thinking about the variables

Once you have a question, you should try to ask it as scientifically as possible. This means identifying the **variables**. When you have a list of variables, you need to decide which variable you are going to change, which variable you are going to measure, and which variables you are going to keep the same to make it a fair test.

There are lots of variables: mass of sugar, volume of water, temperature of water, type of sugar, amount of stirring, time to dissolve.

*So which is your **input variable**, the one you are changing, and which is your **outcome variable**, the one you are measuring?*

Input variable is … temperature. Outcome variable is … time to dissolve. Everything else has to stay the same.

Good, now ask your question in a more scientific way.

Does the time taken for the sugar to dissolve depend on temperature?

Step 3: the risk assessment

You need to think about the experiments you are planning and the risks involved. If you are using chemicals, you need to find out if they are dangerous and what safety precautions to take.

It's pretty safe. I'll follow the lab rules and wipe up any spills. I'll use a kettle rather than a Bunsen burner to heat the water because I'm less likely to burn myself pouring the water.

*Don't forget to write your **risk assessment** down.*

Step 4: equipment and values

You then have to decide how you are going to do the experiments, and what values you are going to use for the input variable, and for the variables you are keeping the same. You will probably have to do some trial experiments to decide if you have all the **equipment** you need, and whether the values you have chosen are sensible.

Start by thinking about the variables. You need to think about the measurements and observations you need to make. This will lead you to the equipment you need.

OK. Input variable is temperature, so I'll need a thermometer. Outcome variable is time, so I'll need a stopwatch. I need to keep the mass of sugar constant, so I'll need a balance, and I'll need a measuring cylinder to measure the water. I'll need a glass rod for stirring. I think I'll do the experiment in a beaker, so I'll need that, and I'll need something to heat the water, so I'll need a kettle. I'm not sure what type of sugar I should use, or the amount of stirring.

*So far so good. Time for some trial experiments. Don't forget to write down any **measurements** and **observations**. They should be there in your final report.*

Some time later.....

Granulated sugar was best, because I could see the crystals better. I decided to put the beaker on a piece of black paper, to help me see when all the crystals had gone. I've decided not to stir, because it makes it too complicated, and to use 50 cm³ of water and 2 g of sugar.

Fine. How many values for the temperature are you going to use? Think about what you are hoping to do with your results. Are you hoping to draw a graph?

I think so. To draw a graph I'll need lots of different temperatures. I'll do five different temperature values: 90 °C, 70 °C, 50 °C, 30 °C and 10 °C.

Is one measurement enough for each temperature?

I suppose not. I'll do two. That's 10 experiments, I'll be there ages.

Step 5: making a prediction

Once you have a plan it is a good idea to make a **prediction**. Sometimes you have nothing to go on, and making a prediction is not possible. However, often you will know something about what you expect to happen. It is best if you can explain why you made your prediction using your knowledge and understanding of science.

The sugar will dissolve quickest at the highest temperature.

Why? Think about it. Look back in your notes. Look up dissolving. Come up with a reason.

Some time later.......

It's all to do with particles. The water is made of particles and the sugar crystals are made of particles. The higher the temperature of the water, the more the water particles move and they hit the sides of the sugar crystals more often, knocking off sugar particles. It takes less time to knock off all the sugar particles if the water particles are moving quicker. I've drawn some diagrams.

Step 6: carrying out

You should have a table prepared to write down your results, because there may not be time once you get going. Do not forget to put titles at the top of each column, along with the units you are using. Sometimes, despite all your planning, it will go wrong. You may have to modify what you were going to do, and repeat parts when things go wrong. The most important thing is to write down what you do.

It was a disaster! I couldn't get the temperature of the water to exactly 90 °C and the sugar took ages to dissolve at 10 °C. I tried to repeat it, but the temperatures weren't exactly the same the second time. I had to do one experiment four times – I kept making mistakes.

Just write down all the problems and don't worry too much. Make a neat copy of your table, but put in the messy one as well – a scientist always includes the original copy.

Turn over for Investigations using experiments (2) on analysing, concluding and evaluating.

Investigations using experiments (2)

Step 7: looking at the data and drawing graphs

Look carefully at your **results**. If your **data** is numbers, then you will probably want to make a chart or graph. You need to make sure it is the correct type of chart or graph, so use a skill sheet or ask someone for advice if you are not sure.

If you repeated experiments, you may be able to **calculate** an **average** (a mean). You can only calculate a mean if the experiments were exact repeats.

There may be other calculations you can do using your results. You may be able to calculate speed, or pressure, or the amount by which something increase or decreased.

However, many investigations do not give results that can be used in calculations. Some investigations will not lead to a chart or graph.

I can't do averages, because my repeats weren't exact repeats. I've got 65 °C and 62 °C, though the others are the same.

Don't worry. Plot all your results on your graph. Do you know what graph to plot?

I think so. The input variable, the temperature, goes along the bottom. The outcome variable, the time, goes up the side. Both variables are numbers that increase continuously, so it's a line graph with a line of best fit. I used the skill sheet.

Good. Are you going to try to plot your times like that, in minutes and seconds? What about turning the times into seconds? They will be easier to plot.

Step 8: looking for patterns and trends

You need to look carefully for **patterns** and **trends** in your results. This is easier if you have made a chart or a graph, because any trend will be more obvious. If you use a line graph, then the line of best fit will show any trends. It is not enough just to draw the chart or graph, you have to describe the pattern or trend in words. This is even more important if there is not a chart or graph.

I've written, 'The higher the temperature the faster the sugar dissolved. This is shown in my graph.'

Step 9: explaining and interpreting

You then need to **explain** what you have found out, using your scientific knowledge and understanding. This is particularly important if you found out something you did not know, or if the investigation turned out differently from what you expected.

But it turned out exactly as I said it would. I've already written about particles and drawn diagrams in my prediction.

You still have to mention it. Your conclusion will not be complete without it.

OK. 'Increasing the temperature increased the speed of the water particles, so they knocked the sugar particles off the crystals more quickly, so the crystals dissolved quicker.'

Step 10: do your conclusions fit with your prediction?

Look back at your prediction, if you made one. Does your **conclusion** fit with your prediction? If it does, you should say so. If it does not, then you may have found out something interesting. At this point, you may be able to make new predictions based on your conclusions.

My conclusion fits with my prediction, but I can't think of any new predictions to make.

Step 11: look at your data again

Evaluating your investigation is difficult. The place to start is your data. Are there any observations or measurements that do not fit into the overall pattern or trend? Point them out and try to explain why they do not fit.

Where do I start? The repeats are not repeats, because I could not get the temperature of the water exactly the same both times. I haven't plotted the result marked with a red ring, because it is so far out. I think I forgot to reset the stopwatch. The times for the higher temperatures are all over the place, so it was hard to decide where the line of best fit should go. This was because it was really difficult to tell exactly when the sugar dissolved, particularly at the higher temperatures, where a second made a big difference.

Step 12: how certain are you?

You need to make a **judgement** about the certainty of your conclusion. If you are not sure, you must say so. Your data may not show the pattern or trend you expected, or the trend may be unclear. Even if all your data fits into the pattern, you need to think whether your conclusion is generally true, or only true for your particular experiments.

I'm sure. The higher the temperature, the quicker sugar will dissolve.

I'm a scientist, so I'm never sure. Your conclusion is only correct for temperatures between 0°C and 100°C, when water is a liquid. Ice and steam will not dissolve sugar. Also, you haven't thought about different amounts of sugar. If the solution is saturated, then no more sugar will dissolve and raising the temperature may not help. Also, your conclusion may hold for liquid water, but it doesn't for other solvents. Sugar will not dissolve in dry cleaning fluid, or many other solvents.

OK. For liquid water, the higher the temperature, the quicker sugar dissolves, provided the solution does not get saturated.

Step 13: suggest improvements to the method

No experiment is ever perfect, so you should be able to think of ways to improve your method.

There are lots of improvements I would like to make. I would like to have a way of keeping the water at a set temperature, like the thermostat in my fish tank at home. Then the repeats would have been repeats and I could have taken an average. I also need a better method of deciding when all the sugar crystals have gone. Perhaps I could use some of the larger, coloured sugar crystals they sometimes serve in restaurants. They might be easier to see, particularly with white paper underneath. I would like to try every 5°C from 5°C to 95°C, but this would only be possible if I had the apparatus for keeping the temperature constant. I would like to have repeated each temperature three times.

3 Investigations without experiments

Working in the real world

I am a geologist. I study rocks because they tell me what happened to the Earth in the past.

I am an epidemiologist. I study the way in which diseases spread in a population.

I am a geneticist. I study genes and the way they are inherited.

I am an animal behaviourist. I study how animals in the wild live together in groups.

I am a cosmologist. I study the Universe.

> Key to understanding these spreads:
>
> black = main text
>
> blue = 'Pippa the pupil'
>
> green = some scientists

Many scientists cannot test their ideas by designing and carrying out experiments in laboratories. Instead, they investigate their ideas by observing and measuring things in the real world.

I am going to investigate whether people with blond hair are more likely to have blue eyes than people without blond hair. My prediction is that people with blond hair are more likely to have blue eyes because both blond hair and blue eyes are due to lack of melanin.

Reducing the differences

When you are doing an investigation in the real world, you cannot control all the variables. For example, if you are studying people then every person is different from every other person. You have to try your best to reduce the differences. You may choose to work on people of a certain age, or a certain gender, or who live in a certain place, or all three. Planets, rocks and stars are all different too.

I don't think reducing the differences is that important for me, because people inherit their eye colour and their hair colour. My main problem will be people who dye their hair. I'll have to leave those out.

Definitions

If you are working in the real world, you have to decide exactly what you are working on. Scientists have to make decisions about how the stars they are studying are different from all other stars, or what type of behaviour is aggressive behaviour in chimps, or which symptoms indicate a particular disease.

I've been to a hairdresser. He gave me these samples of hair. I have made a card with ten hair colours on it. I'll put the whole card up to the person's hair and decide on the closest colour. If it is 1 to 4, then they are blond. The same with the eye colour, but I've made my own card. If the closest colour is 1 to 5, then they have blue eyes.

Sampling

*The larger your **sample**, the more likely it is to reflect the real situation. Your sample should be as large as possible. It is also important that you select your sample without bias. For example, if you are measuring fish then you need to make sure you are catching fish of all sizes. It ruins the investigation if some of the fish are small enough to get through the holes in the net, or large enough to swim away before the net can reach them.*

I've decided how to select my sample. I'll say to people: 'I am doing an investigation into hair colour and eye colour. Please may I look at the colour of your hair and your eyes? I hope you do not mind me asking, but do you dye your hair?' I am going to try to include everyone in the school who has Science lessons when I do. I've asked my teacher. She says that it will be about 400 people.

Analysing your data

Investigating using the real world can generate a lot of data. You need to include all the data in your report, but you need to present it in a way that makes it easy to understand. This can be different for each investigation, and you will have to ask for advice. You then have to decide whether your data supports your original idea or prediction.

I sampled 358 people. 43 were blond, which is 12%. 61 had blue eyes, which is 17%. However, of the 43 blond people, 36 had blue eyes (84%). I think this supports my prediction that having blond hair means you are more likely to have blue eyes.

How sure?

Drawing firm conclusions from real-world situations is difficult. Consider the work of John Snow on the disease cholera. In 1854, John Snow plotted the new cases of cholera on a map. He discovered that they were clustered about a certain public water pump. At that point, all John Snow could say was that the pattern made it likely that the cholera bacteria were in the water from that pump. He then removed the handle from the pump, and the outbreak of cholera stopped. This makes it even more likely that the water from that pump contained cholera bacteria. However, to be sure, he would need to find the cholera bacteria in the water.

I was careful to say that my data only supported my idea. I would need to collect data from other schools in other countries to be sure. Maybe I could do a survey using the Internet!

Secondary data

Often scientists do not collect their own data. Published data collected by other scientists, which can be used in an investigation, is called **secondary data**. One example of this is data collected by the Hubble space telescope. Any scientist can use the data the Hubble telescope collects. There are many sources of secondary data that you could use, for example tables of data on the planets of the Solar System, height and weight charts and weather records.

I wonder if there is any secondary data I could use on hair colour and eye colour? I'll have to do some research.

Half-way house

Often scientists work on organisms in a laboratory rather than in the real world. Moving the organisms from the real world to the laboratory reduces the number of variables, for example, it can mean that all the organisms are in the same environment, or that all have grown up under the same conditions. However, it is still difficult to be sure that what you are measuring is happening because of the experiment. In this situation, scientists use **controls**. A control is a similar organism in similar conditions, which acts as a comparison. For example, if you want to show that light is necessary for photosynthesis, you put one plant in the dark and a similar plant in the light. The plant in the light is a control. If it does not make starch, then there is something wrong with the experimental conditions.

The story of Archimedes

A new image

King Hiero reigned in Ancient Greece. One
day, he decided that it was time for a new look.
Everyone was getting ready to celebrate the feast
day of one of the Greek gods. 'I know what I need
– a brand new crown,' he thought. He sent for the
court goldsmith and gave him a lump of gold to
make the crown.

Crowning glory

Days later, the goldsmith delivered the crown. 'You
look a real treat, your Highness,' he declared.

The next day, the King began to have doubts. Rumours were rife about
the honesty of the goldsmith. The King suspected that the goldsmith
had kept some of the gold and put cheap silver in the crown.

a Which metal did the King
think had been added to
the crown?

Archimedes to the rescue

Hiero sent for his adviser, the brilliant young scientist
Archimedes. 'I am sure you are the person to prove
that the goldsmith is nothing but a common crook.
Just be sure you don't damage the crown because I've
got nothing else to wear for the celebration.'

Back home, Archimedes started to think about this
problem. Solving it would be hard if he could not
damage the crown. He decided to have a bath, and
called a servant to fill one for him. He took off his
clothes and climbed into the bath, not noticing that it
was full to the brim! As he climbed in the water
overflowed onto the floor.

b Why do you think the water overflowed?

That moment, he had an idea. He leapt out of the bath and ran naked
through the marketplace shouting 'Eureka!' which means 'I have found
it!' in Greek.

Archimedes burst into the throne room. (Luckily, a servant was able to
throw him a towel on the way in.) 'Your Majesty, have you got a lump
of gold the same as the one you gave to the goldsmith? I have a way of
testing your crown.'

Archimedes placed the crown on the left-hand side of a balance and then put the lump of gold on the right-hand side. The scales balanced.

'So, my crown is all gold,' the King said, somewhat surprised.

c Why do you think the King was surprised?

'Wait,' explained Archimedes as he filled a large washbasin with water. He carefully lowered the crown into the basin and collected the water that overflowed in a larger basin. He then did the same thing with the lump of pure gold.

'It's pushed out less water than the crown!' cried the King.

'The crown is not made of pure gold,' went on Archimedes. 'If it was pure gold, it would have pushed out the same amount of water. The goldsmith has acted dishonestly. He has used some silver in the crown and kept some of the gold for himself.'

Archimedes explained that silver is lighter than gold. So to make the crown the same **mass**, more silver was needed. The crown took up more space and pushed out more water than the block of gold, because a larger **volume** of silver had been added to make up for the mass of gold the goldsmith had taken out.

d Which do you think is lighter, 1 cm³ of silver or 1 cm³ of gold?

e Why did the crown push out more water than the lump of gold?

'Send for the goldsmith! He is not going to get away with this one,' shouted King Hiero. He thanked Archimedes, saying, 'Keep that other lump of gold.'

Eureka! You have achieved success in science!

Questions

1. Discuss the story of Archimedes with your partner. Copy and complete these sentences together by choosing the correct word from each pair.

   Silver is **lighter/heavier** than gold, so to make the crown the same mass, **less/more** silver was needed. The crown took up **less/more** space and pushed out **less/more** water than the lump of gold because **less/more** silver was needed to replace the gold he took out.

2. Imagine Archimedes weighed the new crown and found that it had a larger mass than the original lump of gold. The goldsmith insists that he has used extra gold to perfect the design.

   a What do you think Archimedes would have done next?

   b How do you think it would be possible for Archimedes to prove that the crown has some lighter metal in it?

Glossary

This glossary contains key words from only the first six units.

addiction   the need to keep taking a drug. The user feels ill unless they can take more of the drug.

alcohol   a legal drug found in beer, wine and spirits. It is produced by yeast during fermentation.

alveoli (singular alveolus)   tiny air sacs in your lungs where gas exchange takes place

antibiotic   a medicine used to fight bacterial infections

antibodies   chemicals produced by white blood cells to kill microbes. Each antibody kills only one type of microbe.

anticlockwise   describes something turning in the opposite direction to the hands of a clock

Archimedes screw   a screw mechanism used to lift water from the ground

artificial insemination   semen is put into the female's vagina through a long tube to make her pregnant without sexual intercourse

balanced turning effect   the effect of two turning forces of the same size acting in opposite directions around a pivot

breathing rate   the number of times a person breathes in and out in one minute

bronchi (singular bronchus)   two main tubes that carry air from the trachea. One bronchus leads to each lung.

bronchioles   small tubes inside the lungs that carry air from the bronchi down to the alveoli

carbon monoxide   a poisonous gas found in cigarette smoke and produced in incomplete combustion

cell division   the process in which one cell divides to form two cells

Celsius scale   a temperature scale in which 0° is the freezing point of water and 100° is the boiling point of water. Celsius temperatures have the unit °C.

clockwise   describes something turning in the same direction as the hands of a clock

competing/competition   trying to get the same food source or other resources as other organisms

conduction   the transfer of thermal energy from one particle to other particles that are touching it

convection   the transfer of thermal energy by moving particles

convection current   the movement in a liquid or a gas caused by the hotter parts rising and the cooler parts falling

correlation   a link between a treatment (such as a medicine) and an effect (such as getting better)

counterbalance   a weight used to balance another force, that stops something falling over

cylinder   part of hydraulic and pneumatic machines. Pistons move inside cylinders.

depressant   a type of drug that slows down the body's reactions and makes the user drowsy and relaxed. Alcohol is a depressant.

desirable features   features that are useful, that you would choose to pass on in selective breeding

displace   an element is displaced when it is removed from its compound by a more reactive element

displacement reaction   a chemical reaction in which an element is removed from its compound by a more reactive element

dissipated   spread around. When energy has been spread about evenly, we say it has been dissipated.

DNA   the substance that genes are made of

dormant 'sleeping'. A dormant organism is not active.

drug a substance that when taken into the body will affect the way that the user thinks or feels

ductile can be pulled into wires

emissions the waste gases from a car exhaust or power station

equilibrium when the forces on an object are balanced, it is in equilibrium

extinct a species that becomes extinct dies out altogether

formal model a model that scientists use to explain what is happening when they can't see it

fungi (singular fungus) a group of organisms, separate from animals, plants and bacteria. Some fungi are microorganisms, like yeast and mould. Some fungi are quite large, like mushrooms and toadstools.

gas exchange the movement of oxygen from the lungs into the blood, and of carbon dioxide from the blood into the lungs. Gas exchange happens across the walls of the alveoli.

gears a machine made from several cogs (wheels) with teeth that turn each other

genes instructions for features which are passed on from parents to offspring

germination the start of growth of a seed. Germination happens when conditions are right.

gravitational potential energy energy stored in an object because the object has been lifted up

group I the elements in the far left-hand column of the periodic table

hallucination seeing things that are not really there. Hallucinations can be caused by drugs.

hallucinogen a type of drug that causes the user to see things that are not really there. LSD is a hallucinogen.

hibernation sleeping through winter to avoid harsh conditions

hydraulic machine a machine that works by transferring pressure through a liquid

hyphae long thread-like tubes that form the main body of many types of fungi such as mould

illegal against the law

immune a person who is immune to a disease-causing microbe does not become ill when they meet that microbe

immune system an organ system that protects the body from infection by microbes

inclined plane a simple machine consisting of a slope, used to make it easier to lift heavy objects

incomplete combustion combustion that is inefficient because not enough oxygen gets to the fuel. It produces poisonous carbon monoxide.

infection an infection is caused when a microbe gets inside the body and grows and multiplies

infrared radiation infrared radiation transfers thermal energy from a hotter object to a cooler object. It is like light but has too low a frequency for us to see it.

inherited passed on from one from generation to the next

interdependent relying on each other. Different species in a habitat are interdependent – they rely on each other for food.

internal energy the sum of the kinetic energy of all the particles inside an object

larynx a part of the trachea which produces your voice. The larynx is also called the voicebox.

lava magma (molten rock) that pours out of a volcano

lever a simple machine for lifting objects, that turns around a pivot

load a force that is moved by a machine. The load is often the weight of an object.

Glossary continued

magma   molten rock

malleable   can be pushed (beaten) into sheets

medicine   a drug that if used correctly can make the body work properly or get better

microbe   a living thing that can only be seen clearly with a microscope. Microbe is another word for microorganism.

micrometre   very small things are measured in micrometres. A micrometre is one-thousandth of a millimetre (a millionth of a metre).

migration   moving long distances to another country. For example, some birds fly to warmer climates in the winter, where it is easier to find food.

milk yield   the amount of milk a cow produces

moment   the turning effect of a force around a pivot. The moment of a force depends on the size of the force and its distance from the pivot.

newton metre   the moment of a force is measured in newton metres

newton per square metre   pressure is measured in newtons per square metre

nicotine   an addictive chemical, found in cigarette smoke

nocturnal   describes animals that are active at night

offspring   new organisms made by reproduction

ovum   egg

ozone   a toxic form of oxygen

passive smoking   breathing in smoke from other people's cigarettes

pathogen   an organism that causes disease

photochemical smog   the haze formed when the sun shines on nitrogen oxides and hydrocarbons in the air. Ozone is produced in the smog by chemical reactions.

physiologist   a scientist who studies how the organs of the human body work

piston   part of hydraulic and pneumatic machines that acts like a plunger, moving in and out of the cylinder

pivot   the point around which a lever turns

placebo   'dummy' tablets or medicine used as a control when testing new medicines. A placebo contains no medicine at all.

pneumatic machine   a machine that works by transferring pressure through a compressed gas

population   the number of organisms of a particular species living in a habitat

potential energy   stored energy. Potential energy usually means energy stored in an object because the object has been lifted up.

precipitate   a solid mass that falls out of a solution

predation   one animal (the predator) hunts and eats another animal (the prey)

pressure   the effect of a force spread out over an area

probability   the chance of an event happening

pulley   a simple machine made from ropes and wheels, which can make it easier to lift something

pyramid of numbers   a diagram that we can draw if we count the number of organisms at each level in a food chain

radiation   the transfer of thermal energy by infrared radiation (which is similar to light but has too low a frequency for us to see it)

reactive   a reactive substance takes part in chemical reactions, usually quickly and releasing lots of energy

reactivity   how reactive a substance is, or how easily it takes part in chemical reactions

reactivity series   a list of metals arranged in order of reactivity with the most reactive at the top

selective breeding   choosing parents with desirable features to produce new varieties of animals or plants that have their desirable features

sexually transmitted disease   a disease that is spread from one person to another during sexual intercourse, for example AIDS

solvent abuse   breathing in the fumes from some glues, paints and lighter fluids. Solvent abuse damages the brain, liver and kidneys.

stimulant   a type of drug that speeds up the body's reactions and makes the user feel they have lots of energy. Caffeine and cocaine are stimulants.

tar   a sticky black substance found in cigarette smoke. It clogs the alveoli and stops the lungs working properly. It can cause cancer.

temperature   this measures the average amount of kinetic energy of the particles in a material

trachea   the tube that leads from the mouth to the lungs. The trachea is also called the windpipe.

transition metals   the elements in the centre section of the periodic table

turning effect   when a force tries to turn an object, the force has a turning effect on the object

unbalanced turning effect   the effect of two turning forces of different sizes acting in opposite directions around a pivot

unit of alcohol   the amount of alcohol found in half a pint of beer, a small glass of wine or a measure of spirits

unreactive   an unreactive substance does not take part in chemical reactions, or does so only slowly

vaccinated   injected with a vaccine so that you become immune to a disease

volcano   a hole in the Earth's crust that magma comes out of

water pressure   the pressure in water. It is caused because water pushes on objects from all sides as the water particles collide with the object.

wheel and axle   a simple machine. The wheel turns in a bigger circle than the axle, which makes some jobs easier.

white blood cell   part of the immune system. White blood cells fight infection by producing antibodies or by swallowing up microbes.

Index

Note: page numbers in **bold** show where a word is **explained** in the text. There are also definitions in the Glossary on page 134-7.

Index continued

Index continued

Index continued

Heinemann Educational Publishers
Halley Court, Jordan Hill, Oxford, OX2 8EJ
a division of Reed Educational & Professional Publishing Ltd
Heinemann is a registered trademark of Reed Educational & Professional Publishing Ltd

OXFORD MELBOURNE AUCKLAND
JOHANNESBURG BLANTYRE GABORONE
IBADAN PORTSMOUTH NH (USA) CHICAGO

© Carol Chapman, Rob Musker, Daniel Nicholson, Moira Sheehan, 2001

First published 2001

ISBN 0 435 57644 5

05 04 03 02
10 9 8 7 6 5 4 3 2

Edited by Ruth Holmes

Index by Indexing specialists

Designed and typeset by Ken Vail Graphic Design, Cambridge

Original illustration © Heinemann Educational Publishers 2001

Illustrated by Graham-Cameron Illustration (Harriet Buckley), Nick Hawken,
Margaret Jones, B L Kearley Ltd (Shirley Bellwood), David Lock, Richard Morris, John Plumb,
Sylvie Poggio Artists Agency (Tim Davies, Rhiannon Powell).

Printed and bound in Spain by Edelvives

Picture research by Jennifer Johnson

Acknowledgments
The authors and publishers would like to thank the following for permission to use photographs:

Cover photos: Solar energy receiver array, Tony Stone Images. **Hippo under water,** Tony Stone Images.
Mushroom-shaped rock pedestal, Science Photo Library/Allan Morgan, Peter Arnold Inc.

1.1c, d Mary Evans Picture Library. **1.2a** Peter Gould. **1.2b** (a) Bruce Coleman/Robert P. Carr, (b), (c) Andrew Lambert, (d) Bruce
Coleman/Iain Sargeant, (e) Bruce Coleman/Judith Clarke. **1.2d** Environmental Images. **1.3b** Holt/Nigel Cattlin. **1.3c** Andrew Lambert.
1.3e Environmental Images/Robert Brook. **1.5a, b** Peter Gould. **1.5d** Science Photo Library/NASA. **1.6a** Science Photo Library. **2.1a**
Science Photo Library/Akira Uchiyimar. **2.1b** Mary Evans Picture Library. **2.1c** Wellcome Trust. **2.1d** (a), (b) Science Photo Library/Dr
Yorgos Nikas, (c) Science Photo Library/Don Fawcett. **2.1e** Mary Evans Picture Library. **2.2a** Sally and Richard Greenhill. **2.2f** Andrew
Lambert. **2.3a** Foto Natura/Frank Lane. **2.3d** Mary Evans. **2.3f** Holt Studios. **2.3h** (a) Holt Studios, (b) Bruce Coleman/Hans Reinhard, (c)
Bruce Coleman/Jane Burton. **2.5b** Oxford Scientific Films/G. I. Bernard. **2.6a** Frank Lane/R. Bird (2 pictures). **2.6b** Avoncroft. **2.6c** Ancient
Art and Architecture. **2.6e** (a) Holt Studios/John Velton, (b) Holt Studios/Nigel Cattlin. **3.2e, f** Gareth Boden (2 pictures). **3.4b** Robert
Harding. **3.4d** Empics (3 pictures). **3.4e** Science Photo Library/John Daughter. **3.4f** Gareth Boden (2 pictures). **3.5g** Gareth Boden. **3.5c**
Bruce Coleman/Pacific Stock. **3.5d** Gareth Boden. **3.6c** Robert Harding. **3.6e** Gareth Boden. **3.7e** Peter Gould. **3.7c** Eye
Ubiquitous/Corbis/R. Obert and Linda Mostyn. **4.1a** Science Photo Library. **4.2b** Geoscience Features/A. Fisher. **4.2c, 4.3a, b, c, d, e, 4.4a,
c** Peter Gould. **4.4d** Beken of Cowes. **4.6a** Science Photo Library/John Mead. **4.6b** Peter Gould. **5.1a** Science Photo Library/Antonia
Reeve. **5.1c** Mary Evans Picture Library. **5.1d** SmithKline Beecham. **5.1b, h** Mary Evans Picture Library. **5.2c** Empics. **5.2d** Action Plus.
5.2e Empics. **5.4a** Science Photo Library/A. Glauberman. **5.4c** DETR. **5.5c** Science Photo Library/Andrew Syred. **5.5d** Science Photo
Library/CNRI. **5.6a** (a) Science Photo Library/CNRI, (b) Science Photo Library/H. C. Robinson, (c) Science Photo Library/Dr P. Marazzi.
5.6c Science Photo Library/Eye of Science. **5.7a** Gareth Boden. **5.7c** (a) Andrew Lambert, (b) Science Photo Library/BSI/P. Beranger, (c)
Science Photo Library/Conor Caffrey, (d) Science Photo Library/TekImage. **5.8a** Science Photo Library/TekImage. **6.1a, c** Science Photo
Library. **6.1e** Science Photo Library/NASA. **6.1f** Stock Market/Otto Rogge. **6.1g** Science Photo Library/NASA. **6.1h** Science Photo
Library/ESA. **6.1I** Science Photo Library/Gordon Sammado. **6.3f** Science Photo Library/Dr Jeremy Burgess. **6.4e, f** Peter Gould. **6.5e** Bruce
Coleman/Jorg and Petra Wagner. **6.5f** Science Photo Library. **6.5g** Empics/Ted Leicester. **6.7a** Peter Gould. **7.6d** Environmental
Images/Daphne Christelis.

Tel: 01865 888058 www.heinemann.co.uk